complete home
STORAGE

By Jeanne Huber and the Editors of Sunset Books

Menlo Park, California

Sunset Books

VICE PRESIDENT, GENERAL MANAGER: Richard A. Smeby
VICE PRESIDENT, EDITORIAL DIRECTOR: Bob Doyle
DIRECTOR OF OPERATIONS: Rosann Sutherland
MARKETING MANAGER: Linda Barker
ART DIRECTOR: Vasken Guiragossian
SPECIAL SALES: Brad Moses

Staff for This Book

MANAGING EDITOR: Bridget Biscotti Bradley
COPY EDITOR: John Edmonds
PAGE PRODUCTION: Susan Paris
ILLUSTRATIONS: Dartmouth Publishing and Tracy LaRue Hohn
PROOFREADER: Meagan C. B. Henderson
INDEXER: Nanette Cardon
PRODUCTION SPECIALISTS: Linda M. Bouchard, Janie Farn
PREPRESS COORDINATOR: Eligio Hernández

10 9 8 7 6 5 4 3 2 1
First printing June 2007
Copyright© 2007, Sunset Publishing
Corporation, Menlo Park, CA 94025.
Third edition. All rights reserved,
including the right of reproduction
in whole or in part in any form.

ISBN-13: 978-0-376-01771-0
ISBN-10: 0-376-01771-6
Library of Congress Control
Number: 2007922070
Printed in the United States of America.

For additional copies of *Complete Home
Storage* or any other Sunset book,
visit us at www.sunsetbooks.com or
call 1-800-526-5111.

COVER
Top left: Courtesy of Rubbermaid. Top middle: Thomas J. Story;
design: Peter O. Whitely. Top right: Thomas J. Story; styling by
Emma Star-Jensen. Center left: Courtesy of Merillat Cabinetry. Center
middle: Courtesy of Maine Cottage. Center right: Thomas J. Story;
interior designer: Kenneth Brown Design. Bottom left: Michele Lee
Willson; styling by Laura Del Fava. Bottom middle: Courtesy of
Exposures. Bottom right: Alex Hayden
PAGE 1: Ken Rice/Corner House Stock Photo

CONTENTS

THE INS AND OUTS OF STORAGE — 4

A World of Clever Solutions — 6

Deciding What Needs to be Stored — 8

Deciding on a Storage Strategy — 10

Maximize Existing Space — 14

Creating New Storage Space — 18

Getting the Most for Your Money — 28

Making Storage Secure — 32

BASIC STORAGE COMPONENTS — 42

Hanging Systems — 44

Shelves — 48

Cabinets — 60

Drawers — 64

Boxes and Bins — 68

ROOM-BY-ROOM   72
STORAGE SOLUTIONS

Entries	74
Living and Family Rooms	80
Kitchens	88
Dining Rooms	124
Bedrooms	126
Bathrooms	148
Home Offices	158
Laundry Rooms	168
Crafts Rooms	176
Attics, Basements, and Garages	180
Resources and Credits	188
Index	191

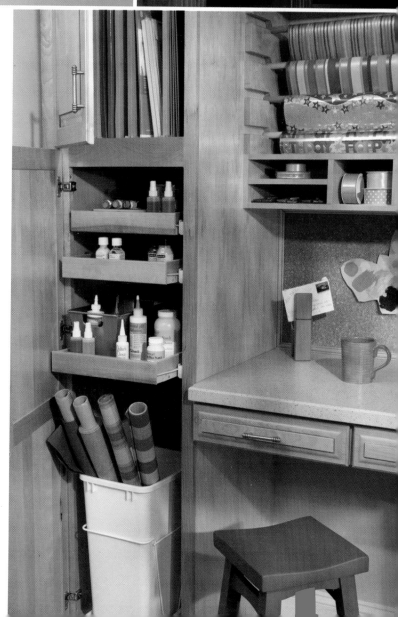

Clothes, tools, books, toys—all the stuff in our lives can sometimes seem just too much. But when it's pared down, organized, and tucked away, a sense of calm prevails. This chapter explores ways to achieve that goal and suggests many ideas to work great storage solutions into your home.

the ins and outs of storage

a world of clever solutions

A.

You may be looking at storage options because you're planning a new house or remodeling a kitchen. Or perhaps you're driven more by frustration: Someone finally tripped on that pile of shoes by the door, or you had to pay a hefty late fee on a bill buried in clutter. Whatever your motivation, this book will guide you to a storage strategy that works for you and then help you carry it out.

Throughout these pages, you will find both ready-made solutions and ones you can craft yourself. If time is short, the quickest option may be to buy a product that works right out of the box. But if you're handy and own even a modest selection of tools, the storage aids you make yourself may cost significantly less and be just as effective.

Either way, great storage is an important finishing touch to a residence. When you can store everything away, you're no longer just camping out. Your house is now home.

Storage space surrounds this built-in couch—even in the armrests, which double as end tables. The bookcase incorporates compartments of various sizes yet still has a tidy look, thanks to the symmetrical design.

B.

C.

A) Good storage solutions often solve multiple problems. This pullout cabinet fits under a counter and has a fold-up table on top. It doubles as a serving cart and additional work surface in a kitchen that's too small for an island.

B) Furniture pieces that are weary or worn but have pleasing lines can still provide useful storage. An old chest, minus most of its drawers, can have a new life as a wine rack.

C) Great storage helps you see what you have and maintain order. In this kitchen, spacious drawers with separate compartments for mixing bowls, pots, and lids replace the deep, dark cabinet typically found under a cooktop.

D) The smaller the space, the greater the need for smart storage. This diminutive entry incorporates a place to sit while you're gearing up, space for shoes, and just enough style to convey a subtle "welcome home."

D.

deciding what needs to be stored

Unless you've moved recently, your home probably holds a lot more stuff than you really need. Paring down is the quickest, least expensive way to solve storage problems. Tackle one room or even one cabinet or closet at a time. Set aside time when you won't be interrupted, and get your mind in a positive mode. Turn on music you love or enlist a friend to help if you know someone who will keep you on track. You can also hire neighborhood teenagers or find expert help through the National Association of Professional Organizers (www.napo.net).

Establish a staging area. Make separate piles for items you will donate or sell, keep, and toss. Divide piles into subcategories as you sort so you handle each item only once. If items need to go to other rooms, place them in labeled boxes for later moving. Don't wander off to put each item away individually.

Is this worth it? Evaluate the true worth of each item as you sort. That coat you haven't worn in two years? The broken chair that's been awaiting repair for three months? Especially with bulky, seldom used items, ask yourself whether the replacement cost exceeds the value of the storage space you'd gain by lightening up.

How to Get Rid of Excess Stuff

While it's tempting to toss everything you don't want into the trash, there are often better options.

■ **Sell.** Match the venue to what you're offering. General household goods, baby gear, and sports equipment move quickly at garage sales. Used clothing fetches higher prices at consignment stores. With collectibles, used building materials, or other specialized items, consider an online auction site, a classified advertisement, or a specialty retailer.

■ **Donate to charity.** Give only what the recipient can use, because charities usually have to pay disposal fees to get rid of true junk. If in doubt, phone before you deliver. Many thrift stores welcome baby items, for example, but don't distribute used strollers or car seats because they may not meet current safety rules. Thrift shops set up to sell scrap fabric may welcome torn or stained clothing, while others do not.

■ **Identify hazardous materials.** You must deal with these responsibly. If solvents, heavy-duty cleaners, and similar materials are still legal to sell and are in their original containers, try to give them to someone who can use them. Otherwise, call your local solid-waste agency or company and ask where to dispose of them. A hazardous-waste disposal  facility is also the best place to take unwanted or outdated prescription drugs. Don't dump medicine down a toilet, as the drugs may pass through waterways. For computers and electronic gear, the environmental program of the Electronic Industries Alliance (www.eiae.org) lists companies that reuse or recycle old high-tech equipment.

One way to improve storage without becoming overwhelmed is to tackle one cabinet at a time. The space under the kitchen sink is a good place to start.

To get better use out of an existing closet, take everything out, sort it, and pare down to what you really use. Then devise a storage strategy that works for what's left. Items from one closet, shown here, broke down into five categories: office, crafts/hobbies, cleaning, clothing, and documents.

deciding on a storage strategy

Do you delight in seeing shoes stacked in neat rows? Or are you more likely to kick off your boots and leave them wherever they land? Keep the answer in mind as you address your storage needs. A strategy that helps you stay organized is a good thing. But if it's too fussy for your style, chances are you won't use it once its newness wears off.

Store like things together. Organize by activity, not type of item. Lids belong next to pots. If you use paper plates only for picnics, keep them with picnic gear, not with your everyday dishes. Match the level of organization to your personal style. If you're a kick-off-the-boots type, it might be enough just to keep all socks together. If you enjoy organizing, sort socks further, perhaps by color or degree of formality.

Store items near place of use. Stash a pail of cleaning supplies in each bathroom. Provide a hamper for dirty clothes in each bedroom. If you're likely to notice and fix a loose button while sorting laundry, store mending supplies nearby. But keep your personal style in mind. In your house, it might make more sense for the sewing kit to be close to the TV.

Neatly lined up on shelves, a shoe collection injects a burst of lively color into a spacious dressing room decorated in a calming off-white. In another person's house, a serene look might be easier to keep up if shoe storage were behind closed doors.

Keep things visible. What you can't see you'll forget you own. Use clear storage containers when possible. Shallow drawers and narrow shelves work better than ones that are too deep. If you have oversized drawers or shelves, consider outfitting them with accessories that help keep items within view.

Note prime real estate. Store your most frequently used items where you can reach them easily. Seasonal equipment, such as camping gear or skis, can go on higher or lower shelves or in areas such as the basement or garage. Your least accessible storage areas are fine for old financial papers and other items that you need to keep but don't actually use.

Recognize that needs change. There's probably no such thing as having too much storage space. But you can invest in components that are too specialized to adapt as your needs change. Will the utensil drawer with compartments perfectly sized for 10 specific tools be of much use after the cork popper breaks and you can't find a replacement of identical shape? If you group things in boxes, leave enough space in each container so you can move items in and out and add new ones. Leave extra room on bookshelves and closet rods too.

While many parents would be thrilled to have an entry that looks this neat, some would find it too messy and might prefer that everything be enclosed.

Match your storage strategy to your personal style. Are you an everything-in-its-place person (above)? Or does a more relaxed organizational style suit you better (left)?

11

Learning from Universal Design

As you plan storage, it pays to think about what will make it most useful over the long term. Features that were once called "handicapped accessible" now tend to be called "universal design" because of a growing realization that everyone's needs change over time—sometimes even from task to task.

Countertop heights. Try to provide work surfaces at different levels.

■ **Kitchen counters.** Typical height is 36 inches, but 30 inches is better for children and people who are seated. For tall people, 45 inches is more comfortable.

■ **Workbenches.** Above elbow height is recommended for precision work, just below for light work, and 4 to 6 inches below elbow height for heavy work.

■ **Home offices.** The computer keyboard should be about 25 inches high for someone 5 feet tall and 30 inches for someone 6 feet tall. See page 161 for details.

These illustrations show what works for an average person (64 inches tall for women and 69 inches for men) and for children. To customize storage for a specific person, measure the reach of one arm while the other is at the person's side.

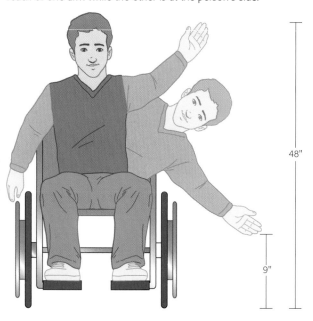

48"

9"

Special hardware. When possible, design storage spaces so that items can move toward you rather than the other way around. Instead of climbing stairs to reach high shelves, for example, outfit the shelves with pull-down hardware so they move within reach. Rather than strain to get into the back of a deep cabinet, install drawers or pullout shelves so the storage rolls forward. Temper this strategy with a financial reality check, however. Some specialized hardware is very expensive; you might not find it worth the added cost.

Wheeled storage. Consider adding one or more storage carts that roll to places where you use what's in them. Besides freeing you from carrying heavy loads, this strategy saves steps and makes cleanup a breeze. For example, if you have breakfast in a sunny dining room, you might stock a small cart with a toaster, coffee maker, sugar, salt and pepper, and whatever else you typically use for the meal.

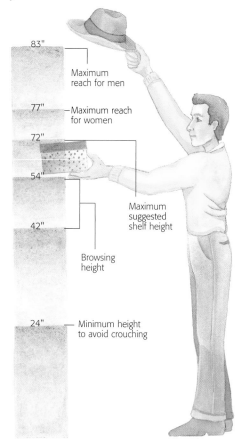

83" — Maximum reach for men

77" — Maximum reach for women

72"

54" — Maximum suggested shelf height

42" — Browsing height

24" — Minimum height to avoid crouching

Designed for a person in a wheelchair, the storage systems in this kitchen work for all people. A breakfast bar doubles as a low countertop. Under the main countertop, some of the base cabinets are actually moveable sections on wheels; they have lower countertops of their own and double as trolleys to transport hot food or dirty dishes. Countertop-height shelves replace standard upper cabinets, which would be beyond the reach of a seated person.

Above the sink, utensils and other gear hang from a long metal rail. Besides keeping the tools visible and making them easy to grab, this system frees up drawer space in base cabinets—prime storage in a fully accessible house.

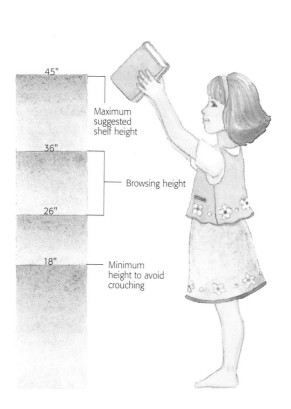

45"

Maximum
suggested
shelf height

36"

Browsing height

26"

18"

Minimum
height to avoid
crouching

maximize existing space

The least expensive, most space-efficient way to add storage is to make better use of what you already have. Besides freeing up space by clearing out clutter, try these ideas for improving existing storage. Many of these strategies are shown in greater detail later in this book.

Add a shelf. Many shelves are farther apart than they need to be, which wastes space and encourages you to stack items so high that they're difficult to retrieve. This is particularly true with garage and pantry systems sold by companies that advertise super-low prices, because including fewer shelves cuts their costs. Luckily, there's a retrofit solution: Add a shelf.

Stack shelves. Where you have both tall and short items to store, consider a stacking shelf unit that spans just part of the space. This lets you double up the short items yet still fit the tall ones on the rest of the existing shelf.

Insert shelf dividers. These work like bookends to separate stacks and ensure that thin items stay upright.

Install pullout shelves. Converting standard shelves to pullout units makes it much easier to reach items stored at the back. Buy kits with the necessary parts, or hire a company that specializes in making these conversions. If you're handy, you can also build sliding shelves yourself using drawer slides, slats of wood or plywood, and pieces of plywood that are slightly smaller than the existing shelves.

Use drawer dividers. You probably already use drawer dividers to keep silverware organized. They're also useful throughout the house for small items such as makeup, office supplies, tools, and art materials. Drawer dividers can be single-piece units or a collection of individual shallow boxes that fit within the space.

BEFORE

Adding a shelf transformed the laundry room above into the well-functioning space below.

AFTER

A.

B.

C.

D.

E.

A) **Stacking shelves** let you keep stacks shorter, so items are easy for you to reach.

B) **If you want to store dishes** in a deep drawer, use dividers to keep stacks from tipping over.

C) **This type of shelf** clips onto a higher shelf and hangs underneath.

D) **Many shelf dividers** are made of wire or wood. These are acrylic, so it's especially easy to see what is in each compartment.

E) **Sliding shelves** allow you to see and reach into the back, so they work better than fixed shelves for storing CDs, tapes, and videos. Purchase or make dividers that keep the containers upright.

Stack drawers. If a drawer is deeper than you need, convert it to a double drawer. It will occupy the same total space but consist of two shallower sections, so more items will stay in view. The top drawer may slide or lift off. Purchase double drawers from cabinet suppliers and hardware companies, or make your own by installing wooden runners inside an existing drawer and setting a smaller drawer or tray on top.

Store on doors. Add storage to cabinet doors as well as doors to rooms and closets. Manufacturers make a variety of units that hook over the top of room-size doors and provide compartments for small items such as shoes, scarves, and cleaning supplies. There are also specialty hooks to hold things like ironing boards. A different array of accessories fits inside cabinet doors.

Add or remove doors. Though cabinet doors might seem like mere packaging rather than actual storage, their presence or absence makes a big difference in how you use the shelves in the cabinets. The contents are always on display with open shelves, so many people use them only to show off a few artfully arranged collectibles. By adding doors, you open up the space for all types of things. Storing items behind closed doors also makes the contents easier to keep clean, as dust won't settle there.

Tuck in a stepstool. If some of your storage space is too high to reach easily, it's essentially useless as a place to keep items you use frequently. To change that, store a stepstool nearby.

Use boxes and bins. Boxes, bins, bags, and other containers help corral small items and keep shelves and drawers neat. Boxes with lids work well for collections you don't use often; choose see-through containers or add labels so you don't forget what's inside. Because bins or cubbies are open at the front, they're better for storing items that you use frequently.

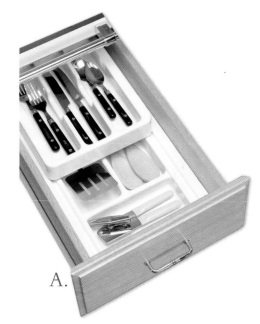

A.

B.

Baskets turn a simple bench into a storage system that could hold boots in an entry or magazines in a living room.

C.

D.

E.

A) **This shallow plastic insert,** called a drawer doubler, keeps more items organized.

B) **This type of double drawer** requires an additional set of drawer slides as well as drawers of suitable depths.

C) **Because cabinet shelves** tend to be recessed slightly, there is usually enough space to add shallow racks on the backs of the doors. If you want deep racks, you may need to make the shelves shallower.

D) **This stepstool folds down** to about 1½ inches thick. It's compact enough to hang from a hook on the inside of a cabinet door or to slip into a gap between a cabinet and a refrigerator. It would also fit in a drawer tucked into the toe-kick space beneath cabinets.

E) **When cabinets rest on countertops,** you need to leave clear space for doors to swing. If the cabinet doors get in the way, remove them or switch them to the sliding, tambour (roll-up), or lift-up type.

creating new storage space

Chances are there are places in your home where you can add storage space. You can probably do this without adding on and without intruding on areas you want to keep open. Houses are built in many different ways, however, so you may need to invest time in studying the possibilities in your home. An architect, builder, or professional organizer can help you identify your options. Here are some ideas to get you started.

Reclaim space under stairs. If you have a multistory house, tuck shelves or cabinets under the stairway. Because stairs are usually at least 3 feet wide, it's difficult to reach all the way in from one side. Work around this by providing access from both sides, or install cabinets that glide out on drawer slides or casters.

A.

Use filler space. Cabinet installers often add filler strips to separate individual sections. Though it's sometimes possible to pry up these strips and use the space behind them, you have more options if you are installing new cabinetry. Instead of a filler strip, you can leave a slot to store cookie sheets, trays, or cutting boards. In a family room or a laundry, a folded-up card table or a stepstool might fit.

Climbing up the back side of a staircase, ascending shelves hold books and other small objects yet leave the space under the stairway open.

B.

C.

D.

E.

A) When storage systems are installed under stairs, tiny triangles of space at the top and bottom often go unused. In this house, a wine cubby makes use of the upper space.

B) Even the ceiling under a staircase can be outfitted for storage.

C) Built-in cabinetry is not the only way to create storage under a staircase. Simple shelves equipped with boxes and bins also work nicely. You could even skip the shelves and just stack sturdy boxes.

D) A narrow space also works well for hand towels.

E) Cabinet companies offer pullout shelves that fit into gaps as narrow as 3 inches. They must be installed along with the cabinets and can't be added later. Dressing up the front panel with molding gives cabinets a look that resembles freestanding furniture.

Use the toe-kick. Most base cabinets rest on a frame that's about 4 inches tall and slightly shallower than the cabinets. This creates a front recess known as a toe-kick, which keeps you from bumping your toes when you work at the counter. By building a shallow drawer into the toe-kick, you can preserve the benefit without wasting the space. Toe-kick drawers are easy to install along with the cabinets. Adding them to existing cabinetry is nearly impossible unless the cabinets are moved, perhaps in preparation for a floor repair or a remodeling project.

Think like an architect. Instead of fitting storage space into the architecture of your house, you can use compartments as architecture. A block of cabinets or shelves works well as a room divider, creating the effect of walls where there are none. You can also use storage units to increase a sense of separation between adjoining rooms. This technique might be useful if you have a home office that needs more isolation from the rest of the house or if you have a bedroom that opens directly off your kitchen or living room.

A.

In a house with an open floor plan, storage units and a change in elevation create a clearly defined living room. From the kitchen, the storage area looks low, which keeps the cook connected to activity in the living room. But from the living room, the cabinetry looks taller, creating a semi-enclosed, cozier feeling.

B.

C.

A) Toe-kick drawers in kitchens or bathrooms are good places to store big, flat things, such as pans and hand towels.

B) Floor-to-ceiling storage units thicken a wall with a doorway, increasing the sense that the spaces on either side are different realms. In this house, the wall of books also helps muffle sound.

C) If you sometimes want spaces connected and sometimes want them separate, a storage cabinet equipped with a pull-down shade or door may be the answer. Between a kitchen and a dining room, this setup allows guests and cooks to mingle while the meal is prepared. When the food is ready, the cabinet works as a pass-through serving area. Then the shade goes down to hide the kitchen mess while everyone dines.

D) In a bathroom, a judiciously placed wall creates an alcove for a pedestal tub and provides a base for inset shelves next to the sink.

D.

Use high walls. Above closets and upper cabinets and on walls above stairways, considerable potential storage space often goes unused. In open areas, you can simply add shallow shelves and fill them with decorative items that you don't need to reach very often. You may need to add a lip to keep items from tumbling off. Over closets and cabinets, consider building a cubby into the wall rather than trying to get access through the closet. Though it's usually possible to add a high shelf or two over the rod, once you leave room for getting items up and down from the shelves, the actual storage shrinks. But if you can access this space from the room itself, the shelves can extend the full depth because you don't have to maneuver through the closet.

Tap into a corner. In your kitchen, laundry, bathroom, or elsewhere, do cabinets meet in a corner where it's hard to reach into the back or where that space is blocked off? Though you can buy lazy Susans or other special shelves that make corner cabinets more useful,

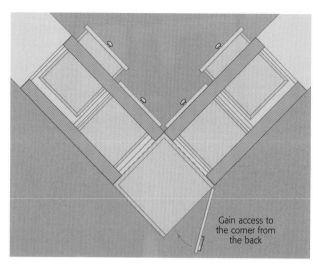

Gain access to the corner from the back

the most elegant solution is to open up a wall behind the cabinet and cut through part of the cabinet's back panel to gain access from an adjoining room.

Fold down or up. Where you want storage but also need clear floor space, systems that fold up and down may be the best option. Some solutions are ready-made, while others may require a clever custom design.

A wall bed is the quintessential fold-down storage unit. Often designed to include compartments for bedding or other items, it's commonly called a Murphy bed after its original patent holder. Today, cabinetmakers sometimes use wall bed hardware as the mechanism for fold-down desks, hobby areas, and workbenches.

A.

B.

C.

D.

A) Over a walk-in closet in a children's bedroom, there is enough space for a loft that stores a huge collection of stuffed animals and still leaves room to play or read.

B) Wired for a computer and battery chargers, a fold-down desk puts household electronic gear where it's easy for grownups to use but safely away from curious tykes.

C) You can use out-of-the way spots to display collectibles. Just be sure you have a way to dust the items periodically.

D) Cabinets flanking a stove pull triple duty, providing storage, work surfaces, and heat-safe counters. When the drop-down doors serve as work surfaces, the cook pulls out drawers underneath to add stability. Hot pots can be set on the doors, thanks to metal cladding.

Claim areas under upper cabinets. It's a shame not to use this prime space. Consider a narrow fixed shelf, cubbyholes, a bar rack, a pull-down shelf, a bulletin board, or even simple hooks. A pull-down shelf might hold a stain-removal guide in a laundry room or a dictionary in a home office. In a bathroom, a divided tray that pulls down under a medicine cabinet can hold hairclips, nail polish, or other small items.

Build storage into furniture. Think of all the places where you use only the top surface of furniture but could gain useful space below. Tables, beds, and couches are among the possibilities. You'll have the most options when you are buying new furniture, but there are some retrofit possibilities too. For example, you can add a shelf to most tables by screwing support rails between each pair of end legs and then resting a shelf on those.

Use space between studs. Most houses in the United States are supported by a skeleton of 2 by 4s or 2 by 6s. On exterior walls, insulation fills the spaces between these studs. But on interior walls, the gaps are usually empty save for an occasional electrical wire or water pipe. By carefully cutting through the drywall or lath and plaster covering the studs, you can open up this space and use it for shelving, a recessed medicine cabinet, a built-in ironing center, a broom closet, or other shallow storage systems.

A.

B.

A **built-in couch** has drawers along the base, as well as a bookcase built into one end. Substituting for an end table, the bookcase gives people sitting on the couch a place to set a coffee cup or a newspaper.

A) A pull-down kitchen shelf can support a knife rack, a cookbook, a spice rack, or even a message center.

B) In a kitchen, a narrow fixed shelf under an upper cabinet makes a great spot for spice jars or boxes of tea bags.

C) The seat of this garden bench lifts up, revealing hidden storage for coiled hoses. Mesh at the bottom allows wet hoses to air-dry. Get the construction plans for this bench at www. sunset.com.

D) Store collectibles safely away from dust by keeping them under glass, as this coffee table does.

E) Walls alongside staircases make good candidates for inset storage. Bookcases can be rectangular or have a shape that climbs in step with the treads.

F) In a child's room, inset shelves create cubbies for toys and other treasures and leave floor space open for play.

How to Open Up Space Between Studs

Inset storage is a good solution on interior walls where no wires, pipes, or ducts are in the way. The directions here cover situations in which the storage system fits between studs or is in a wall that doesn't support the weight of a higher floor or the roof. (On load-bearing walls, the steps are more complicated.) If you cut studs, you may need a building permit.

1 Find and mark studs (see Finding Hidden Studs, below). With the help of a carpenter's level, outline the storage unit's position plus 1¾ inch on the top and on the bottom, and ¼ inch on each side. Try to align one side of the opening along the inside edge of a stud.

2 To make sure wires or pipes aren't in the way, drill a ¼-inch hole through the drywall between each set of studs, snake through a bent coat hanger, and twirl it around. If it hits nothing, cut a peephole about 4 inches across and peer inside.

3 If everything is clear, cut through the drywall with a drywall saw or a jigsaw. Switch to a utility knife where a stud is underneath. Pull off the loose drywall.

4 With a small handsaw or a jigsaw, carefully cut any stud in the way. (If the saw blade binds, the wall might be load-bearing. Stop and reevaluate.) As you remove the wood, gently pry it from the drywall on the back so you don't have to repair the other side of the wall.

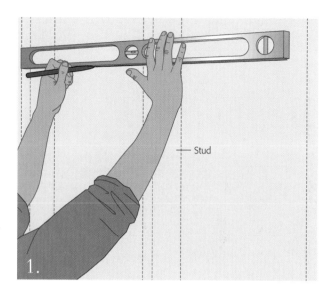

Stud

1.

5 Cut framing lumber to fit gaps between studs at the top and bottom of the opening. Add cripple studs to support the ends and middle. Attach the pieces with 3-inch screws.

6 If there is no stud under a vertical edge of the drywall, cut a 2-by-4 trimmer stud to fit between the upper and lower framing. Also cut short blocking pieces. Screw the blocking into place, then fasten the trimmer stud. Use 3-inch screws. If you need to patch the drywall, fasten it to the new framing with 1⅝-inch screws.

7 Install shelves or a cabinet using screws long enough to bite at least 1 inch into the framing.

Finding Hidden Studs

To locate studs hidden by drywall, use an electronic stud finder or tap on the wall and listen for the sound to shift as you move from areas that are hollow to ones where wood lies underneath. To be certain, drill a tiny confirmation hole before you proceed. Once you locate one stud, the others are easier to find because their edges are usually 14½ or 22½ inches apart (or 16 and 24 inches measured from centerline to centerline).

2. Rotate bent wire behind drywall

3. Saw along stud if possible

Drywall saw

Pilot hole

4. Hand saw

5. Framing lumber

Cripple studs

6. Blocking

Trimmer stud

Blocking

7.

getting the most for your money

You can spend a lot on storage systems and buy style, convenience, and plenty of capacity. You can also solve your storage problems relatively inexpensively, with more style than generations of college students have achieved with concrete blocks and bare pine boards.

If you need free or super-cheap storage, start by reusing boxes or other containers that come with the purchases you make, or buy and install simple hooks. After those, the least expensive type of storage is usually shelving. Cabinets with shelves are next, followed by cabinets with pullout shelves. Cabinets with drawers cost the most.

Beware of selecting a storage system by price alone. Flimsy shelving that bends out of shape or drawers that don't slide freely once full are no bargain. On the other hand, if all you want to store are jars of spices, you don't need shelving that can support bricks.

This garage storage system hangs from a heavy-duty steel rail that can support up to 1,750 pounds over 56 inches. The same manufacturer makes a similar system that holds just 300 pounds. That rail is a few inches shorter, but the big difference is that it is aluminum. If you didn't think to ask, you might never notice this significant difference in materials.

Handsome wooden wine-crate boxes work wonderfully as filing boxes. Orient letter-size files crosswise and legal-size folders lengthwise. Flat lids allow you to stack boxes. Cutout handholds make them easy to transport.

Load capacity. Before you buy storage systems with shelves or drawers, find out what weight they can carry. Some manufacturers state this as weight per square foot. Others cite total weight per shelf or drawer. The difference is significant. For example, shelves loaded with hardbound books must be strong enough to support at least 40 pounds per square foot and maybe 50 pounds if the books are unusually large. You can't use a 12-inch-wide shelf 30 inches long that can hold a load of 40 pounds, because that averages out to 16 pounds per square foot. For more information about the load-carrying capacity of shelves, see page 50.

Adaptability. Manufacturers often tout shelves that are fully adjustable. Even though people rarely change the way shelves are arranged, the marketing push behind this option does reflect one of the basic truths about storage: Needs do change over time. It's important to invest in solutions that you can use in a variety of ways and expand if necessary. You'll probably never regret lining a garage wall with shelves, a few closed cupboards, and a stack of large bins. But mismatched plastic shelving units inevitably wind up as clutter. Instead of a small rack that stores the five gardening tools you own today, look for a system that you can expand as your tool collection grows. Systems you build yourself from common materials may be easiest for you to adapt.

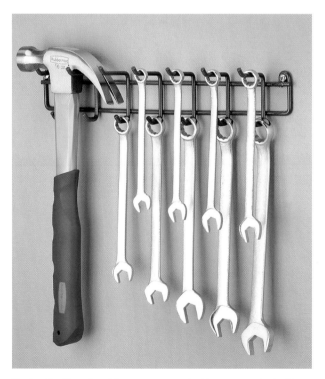

Tool collections tend to grow as you tackle more projects. If your set is small today, a tiny rack like this may seem sufficient. Buying one or more spares, however, allows you to expand your storage system as you add tools.

> ### Helpful Hint
>
> Depending on where you shop, you may find it easy or nearly impossible to learn specifics about the strength of various storage systems. Go when the store is not busy. If a clerk can't look up the information you need, note the manufacturer. Check its Web site or call its customer service department.

Finding Great Storage at Bargain Prices

If you are on a tight budget or don't want to invest in storage systems that you might not be able to use after a move, consider buying pre-owned units. It may take some sleuthing to find what you like, but if you stick with it, you're likely to wind up with shelves, cabinets, or other solutions that are of better quality yet less expensive than what you find new at outlets focused on offering bargain prices.

Used store fixtures. Buy used store fixtures for basements, garages, workrooms, or other spaces where you need heavy-duty shelving. Gondolas, which have cantilevered shelves on one or both sides, are especially useful. They fit together without tools, and because they are freestanding, you can disassemble and move them without needing to patch walls. The steel shelves are fully adjustable and strong enough to support pretty much anything. Because there are no poles in front or angled brackets at the back, you can place several units next to each other and easily store long material, such as skis or lumber. Gondolas typically come with a pegboard back, but you can replace it with thin plywood or another sheet material. You can also paint the shelving to give it a less industrial look.

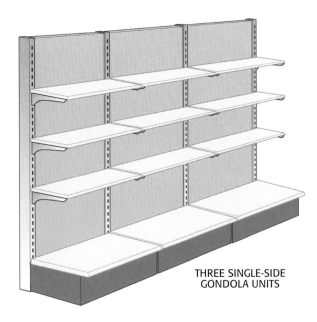

THREE SINGLE-SIDE
GONDOLA UNITS

Salvaged office furniture. Because companies come and go with astounding frequency, salvaged office furniture is available at bargain prices in many areas of the country. Look in the phone book under "Office equipment—used" for desks, file cabinets, and bookcases. Besides using them in a home office, you can put them to good use in children's bedrooms, laundry areas, and workshops. If you outfit drawers with hanging files, they're ideal for storing many craft materials, such as specialty papers, as well as appliance repair manuals, children's school mementos, and recipe collections. Desktops tend to be made of particleboard, which is quite heavy, so consider buying only base units and topping them with a hollow-core door, which is inexpensive and lightweight.

Used building materials. Stores that specialize in used building materials are another great source for inexpensive storage units, as well as lumber and molding that you can use to build custom shelving or cabinets. If you hire someone to do the work, the added time you spend searching for just the right materials may cancel out your savings. But you'll still have the satisfaction of reusing supplies that ought not be thrown away, and you may wind up with vintage-looking pieces that you treasure. The inventory at stores that sell used building materials often changes quickly. One day you may discover nothing appealing. On the next visit, you may find gorgeous solid-wood cabinets salvaged from a school slated for demolition.

Find local sources in the phone book under "Building materials—used" or under "Architectural salvage." Also check local classified advertisements. Because it's expensive to dump unwanted cabinetry in a landfill, more and more contractors and even homeowners are trying to find new homes for the materials they rip out in preparation for remodeling.

Most of this kitchen remodel was done with used building materials or other salvaged items.

Assemble different components to create substantial storage systems. This bookcase, for example, could be made with two narrow units and one that's a little wider and taller. Finishing touches include molding, furniture feet, and fresh paint.

Shop secondhand stores. Secondhand-furniture stores and garage sales can be good sources for tired storage pieces at great prices. Look for furniture that has a shape or another design feature you like. With fresh paint and sometimes a shelf or two, you can transform these pieces into functional, attractive storage.

making storage secure

When you store things away, you want them to be in good condition when you need them. Your storage solutions should ensure that nothing harms your items and that your items harm no one. Depending on what you're storing, that may mean keeping out young children or pets, barring bugs or rodents, or preventing damage in an earthquake or a fire. Fortunately, a little foresight can go a long way toward preventing problems.

Many storage systems must be fastened to a wall. If you don't do it right, shelves and cabinets can pull loose. The higher or heavier the storage, the more secure the connection needs to be.

Spice racks or shelves for shoes can be screwed to drywall, provided you first install anchors. Drywall is too crumbly to hold fasteners directly. To determine which anchors will work for your project, add the weights of the storage unit and its contents, then divide by the number of fasteners. Buy anchors rated for at least that load, as the items on the shelf might change over time.

Heavier storage units need to be fastened directly to wall studs. Use long screws, ideally 3 inches, because the holding power depends on how many threads are within the wood. Use thick screws with heads that are flat on the back. Drywall screws are too brittle, and their bugle-shaped heads don't hold as well.

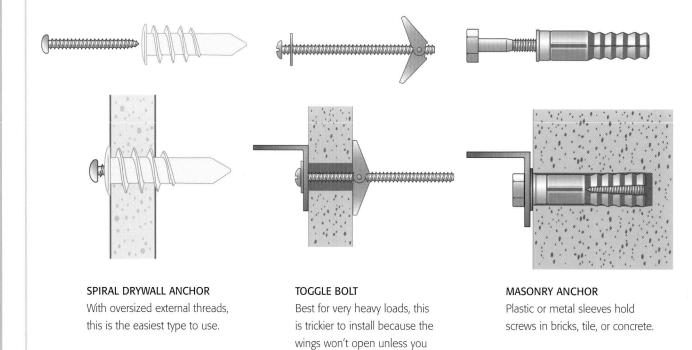

SPIRAL DRYWALL ANCHOR
With oversized external threads, this is the easiest type to use.

TOGGLE BOLT
Best for very heavy loads, this is trickier to install because the wings won't open unless you keep tension on the screw.

MASONRY ANCHOR
Plastic or metal sleeves hold screws in bricks, tile, or concrete.

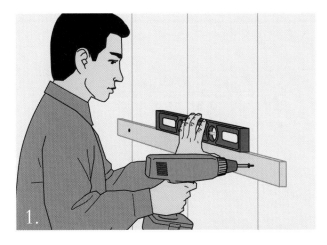

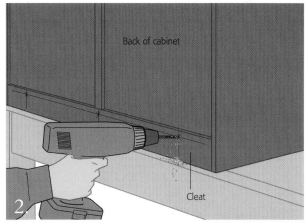

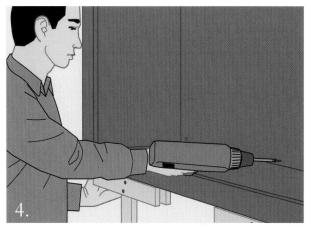

Back of cabinet

Cleat

1.

2.

3.

4.

How to Mount Cabinets

The main challenge is keeping the cabinet in position while you fasten it to studs. You also need to make sure that the part you're fastening is strong enough and that the fasteners penetrate into wood, not just drywall. Some cabinets come with a two-part rail system. You screw one section to the wall at studs and then lift the cabinet, with the other rail attached, into place. If there is no attachment system, use the method shown here.

1 Begin at the bottom. Mark the location where the cabinet will go, then locate and mark studs within that area. Attach a temporary cleat just under the bottom of the cabinet location, using a screw at each stud. Make sure the cleat is level.

2 Most cabinets have cleats on the back that span the top and bottom. Mark stud locations on these and

drill pilot holes. (If there are no cleats, cut boards to fit inside the cabinet and then nail them on through the sides.) Drill high enough to allow clearance for your drill inside the cabinet (see step 4).

3 Professionals use adjustable lifts to hold the front of the cabinets in position temporarily, but you can improvise with homemade T-shaped braces made from framing scraps. Lift the cabinet onto the cleat against the wall and slip the T braces in place. Check that the cabinet is level and plumb.

4 To attach the cabinet to the wall, drive screws through the pilot holes in the upper and lower cleats. In most cases, use 3-inch screws.

Protecting Against Earthquake Damage

Earthquakes occur most often in the West, but the entire country is vulnerable. Because there's no way yet to predict when a quake might hit, the only way to minimize injuries and damage is by preparing properly.

Keep storage units from toppling. Tall bookcases, entertainment centers, and armoires easily topple during a quake and are a leading cause of injury. Secure them to wall studs with metal L brackets and long screws. Then fasten the brackets to the top or to the sides of the unit where they won't be too noticeable. Don't screw into a flimsy back panel.

Protect stored items from damage. You can't keep things you store from being heaved up and down in an earthquake, but you can keep them from being tossed across the room or spilled on the floor.

■ **Straps.** Computers and other large electronic gear should be secured to shelves or studs. Use flexible straps with buckles or hook-and-loop fasteners so you can move the equipment when necessary.

■ **Latches.** These keep cabinet doors shut. Replace magnetic catches, which rattle loose. Latches, which have parts that interlock, may open with the turn of a handle or the push of a button. Hooks and sliding bolts also work. Latches used to baby-proof kitchens

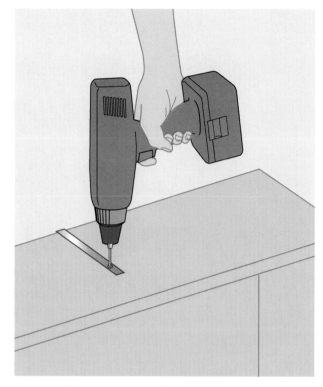

ATTACHING TALL BOOKSHELVES TO THE WALL

are another option, but while new parents quickly master them, people without kids may consider them a hassle.

■ **Putty.** Keep things from sliding off open shelves. Putty made for this purpose allows you to temporarily "glue" collectibles in place. Or attach adhesive-backed hook-and-loop fasteners.

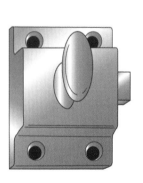

CABINET LATCH

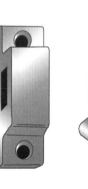

PUSH-BUTTON LATCH

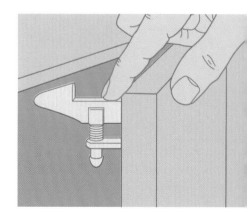

CHILD-SAFETY LATCH

Molding that creates a lip can keep stored items from sliding off a shelf or cabinet during an earthquake, but things might still bounce over the lip. Instead, store heavy or especially valuable objects on lower shelves or in cabinets with latches.

Spring-loaded turn latches keep these vintage cabinets closed securely even in an earthquake. Reproduction hardware is virtually identical to the original.

Storing Emergency Supplies

In addition to securing your storage systems against earthquakes, assemble and store a disaster supplies kit that could sustain your family for four to seven days. Keep it in a watertight container, such as a plastic garbage can. Experts say to store the emergency container outdoors, but for some people that's not a safe option. If you do decide to store it in your garage, place it near the door.

- portable radio (wind-up type, if possible)
- flashlight (wind-up type, if possible)
- extra batteries (if needed)
- first aid kit and handbook
- prescription medications
- emergency cash
- car keys
- important phone numbers
- copies of personal identification
- matches and charcoal
- camping stove
- personal necessities (diapers, hearing aids, spare glasses, toothbrush)
- ready-to-eat food, including high-calorie snacks
- manual can opener, if needed for the food
- bottled water (at least 4 gallons per person)
- warm clothes
- tarp
- heavy-duty plastic garbage bags
- 5-gallon bucket with tight-fitting lid (for waste)
- toilet paper
- hand sanitizer gel
- basic nonelectric tools: hammer, saw, pry bar, wrench, pliers
- several pairs of work gloves
- pet food and leashes
- comfort items (crayons, paper, teddy bear)

Storing Hazardous Materials

If you store pesticides, powerful cleaning solutions, solvents, gasoline for a lawn mower, or other hazardous materials, you must devise a storage method that makes them inaccessible to young children. You also need a system that will prevent dangerous chemical reactions if there are spills, a fire, or an earthquake.

Check labels to determine specific storage requirements. Some hazardous materials need to be kept where there is good ventilation so dangerous fumes don't build up. Some products change consistency or effectiveness if they become damp or are stored where temperatures are too low or high.

■ **Store as little as possible.** Before you buy any hazardous product, investigate whether a less toxic alternative exists. If you must use something that poses a health or fire risk, ask neighbors if they have leftovers that you can use. When you do buy these products, select a size that matches your needs. Store leftovers in their original containers, which are labeled with the safety information that you will need when you use the remainder.

■ **Separate acids and alkalis.** To prevent a dangerous chemical reaction in case of spills, keep highly acidic products separate from materials that are highly alkaline. Chlorine bleach, washing soda, and ammonia are alkaline. Toilet bowl cleaners, concrete cleaners, wood brighteners, and rust removers are acidic.

■ **Banish flammables.** If you store a large quantity of oil-based finishes or other highly flammable materials, consider keeping the containers in a weather-tight, locked cabinet away from your house. This way, if a fire does break out, your stored items won't make it more intense. Most oil-based finishes withstand freezing, but water-based formulas tend to break down if they are repeatedly frozen and thawed. They should not be kept in an outdoor cabinet if you live where winters are cold.

Metal safety cabinets include vent holes that allow smelly vapors to escape. Consult the fire department for local regulations. Industry-approved units generally involve a metal duct leading outdoors from a bottom vent, as chemical vapors tend to be heavier than air. Replacement air comes through a top vent.

A lockable cabinet is a good place to keep household chemicals away from children.

Build a Safety Cabinet

It may seem surprising, but if you store flammables in your house or garage, you can build a wooden storage cabinet for them that meets the same specs as $500-plus industrial-style metal safety cabinets do. It's possible because wood insulates from heat, while metal conducts it. The National Fire Protection Association specifies that wooden safety cabinets need to be made of 1-inch exterior plywood, with rabbeted (grooved) joints fastened in two directions with screws. If there are two doors, you need to overlap them by at least an inch. And you need to put a 2-inch-deep pan at the bottom to contain spills. With all that, the cabinet meets federal rules for workplace safety cabinets. Even if the room is on fire, the cabinet should keep the finishes from bursting into flames for 10 minutes—enough time for everyone to get out of the house before the fire really gets hot.

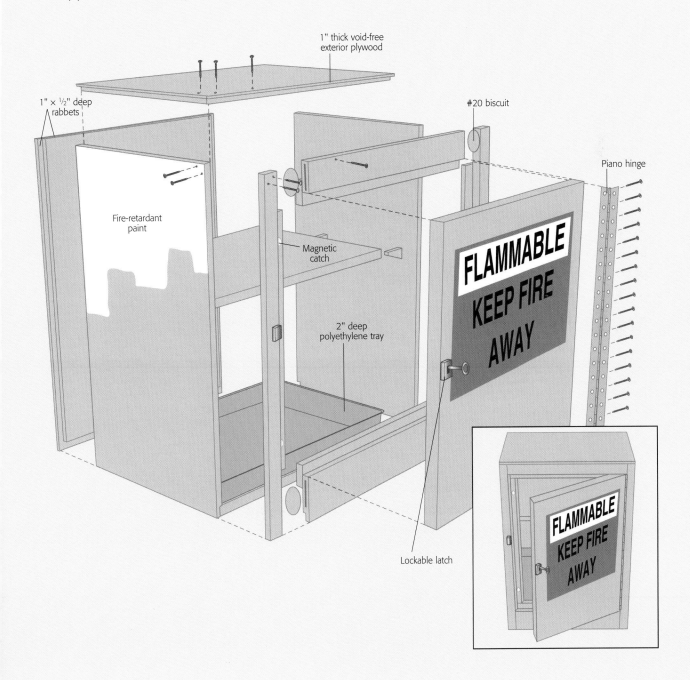

1" thick void-free exterior plywood

1" × ½" deep rabbets

#20 biscuit

Piano hinge

Fire-retardant paint

Magnetic catch

2" deep polyethylene tray

FLAMMABLE KEEP FIRE AWAY

Lockable latch

FLAMMABLE KEEP FIRE AWAY

Baby-Proofing

Young children delight in playing with pots and pans, and there's usually no reason to stop them. They can't hurt the pots, and the pots rarely hurt them. But many situations aren't so benign.

■ **Add latches.** When you must keep children out of cabinets or drawers, use latches that are too complicated or require too much strength for children to open. Hardware stores and shops that specialize in baby items sell a variety of these.

■ **Store out of reach.** Because childproof latches don't work if you forget to close doors or drawers, don't depend on hardware alone. Store powerful cleaners and other dangerous products on a high shelf or in a high cabinet, not under the kitchen sink.

■ **Check lids.** If you store toys in a toy box, dirty clothes in a hamper, or music in a piano bench, make sure the lid can't slam shut. Replace standard hinges with lid supports, which hold a lid open and then slowly lower it when pressure is applied.

A) This flexible plastic catch hooks onto a tab mounted inside the cabinet box, allowing the drawer to open just far enough for an adult to push down to release it. The parts stick on, so you don't have to worry about marring the cabinet.

B) This latch swivels off, so it's ideal for a home where young children are present only occasionally.

C) Instead of latching each side of a pair of doors separately, you can use a single push-button lock to secure them both.

Besides lid supports that keep the top from slamming shut, this toy box has a built-in gap between the lid and the front so fingers can't get caught. Tall bookcases like this should be secured to the wall with brackets, hidden behind the crown molding at the top.

A.

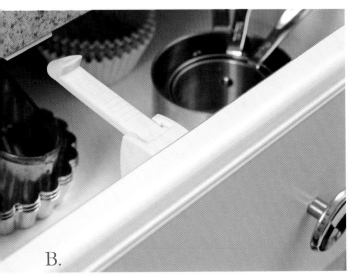

B.

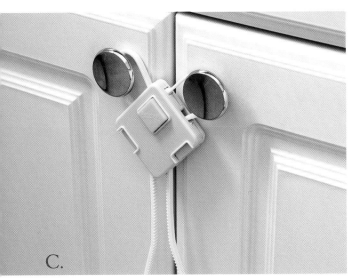

C.

Keeping Out Pests

It's a sad day when you unpack ski clothes the night before a trip to the slopes, only to discover that tiny caterpillars have chewed holes in your woolen hats or that an ant colony has claimed them as nest material. Several strategies can help keep stored items safe from insects, rodents, and other pests.

■ **Clean first.** Some of the most troublesome pests seek out stored items that contain traces of body oils and other substances that are potential food, but they are uninterested in clean items. Storing only clean items is the most effective way to protect clothing from the moth species that eat tiny holes in fabric during their caterpillar stage.

■ **Use pest-resistant containers.** Keep stored items, especially food and things you rarely use, in containers with tight-fitting lids. Not only does this keep out pests, but it also contains any that sneak in along with your purchases.

■ **Do regular checkups.** Go through your stored items periodically so you can deal with any pest problems before they spiral out of control. Empty and clean clothes closets once or twice a year. Go through pantries more frequently and purge whatever has become stale. In garages and basements, besides checking what you have stored, also clean under and around any cardboard boxes, which make ideal hiding spots for insects and even rodents.

Helpful Hint

Don't count on cedar to protect fabrics from the caterpillars of clothing moths. Though freshly milled cedar does contain natural moth repellents, the scent dissipates over time. Even a fresh scent might not be strong enough to work.

Protecting Stored Heirlooms

Take extra care when you store family treasures, as most aren't replaceable. And because they tend to be stored for long periods, a lot of pest or moisture damage may occur before you notice it and are able to intervene.

■ **Choose a storage area.** This should be within the main part of your house rather than in the attic, basement, or garage, if possible. Aim for moderate temperature with moderate or low humidity. Don't store heirlooms next to a heater or in bright light.

■ **Clean or air out.** Wash items before you store them. Don't try to make antiques look new, but do remove food debris or pet dander that might attract insects or other pests. You can vacuum many items, but to prevent damage, reduce the vacuum suction by opening the vent on the wand and covering the tip with nylon net or cheesecloth. In addition, cover fragile fabrics with a piece of window screen before you vacuum.

■ **Use archival-quality storage containers.** These are important for vulnerable items. Standard cardboard boxes and other packing materials contain acids and other ingredients that may cause irreversible damage to some materials, especially paper (including photographs) and fabric. If you're worried about insects or other pests, consider plastic boxes with snap-on lids. But make sure the boxes are made of polypropylene, which carries the number 5 in the plastic recycling symbol. Don't use

boxes made of polyvinyl chloride (number 3), as it releases chemicals that damage many materials. Other safe plastics, which you may find in storage products other than boxes, are high- and low-density polyethylene (numbers 2 and 4) and a form of polyester known as polyethylene terephthalate, or PET (number 1). Polyester does carry a static charge, however, so it shouldn't be used to store materials such as artwork done in chalk, which might lift.

■ **Special needs.** Learn about storage requirements for specific materials. Before you dismantle an old photo album on the assumption that it would be better to transfer the prints to new archival-quality pages, for example, check what the National Archives (www. archives.gov) has to say. For many other materials, a good source is the American Institute for Conservation of Historic & Artistic Works (aic.stanford.edu). There you can also learn how to contact a professional conservator if you need additional help.

> **Helpful Hints**
>
> ■ Pad the folds in textiles or leather with white cotton or acid-free tissue paper to prevent creases, which add stress and may cause cracks or tears.
>
> ■ Scan or photocopy important papers before you store them, in case they do become damaged. Photograph bulkier items.

Storage Envelopes

Professional conservators often store heirlooms in bags made of Tyvek. Instead of buying new bags from an archival-storage company, consider reusing large express shipping envelopes. They are also made of Tyvek, though with an anti-static coating not found on archival materials. The coating is water soluble. To keep it from leaching onto your heirlooms, rinse the envelopes first in cold water. Let them air-dry, as a dryer can melt Tyvek.

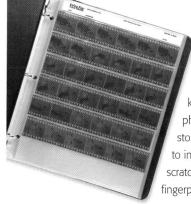

Negatives sometimes produce acidic gases as they age, so you should keep them separate from photographs. Clear negative storage sleeves allow you to inspect the film without scratching it or marring it with fingerprints.

A.

B.

C.

A) One pleasure of owning historical photographs is displaying them in your house. However, this makes them vulnerable to fading from sunlight or artificial light. Covering the pictures with plastic that filters out ultraviolet light reduces this damage. The best solution is to duplicate the image and put the copy on display. Store the original in an archival box, away from light. Pre-1980s color photographs are especially vulnerable and are probably already faded. But they can be scanned into a computer and digitally enhanced to near-original colors, then printed onto more stable photographic paper. Avoid using computer printer paper for this because prints fade very quickly.

B) Use archival storage boxes to store heirloom textiles. Constructed from acid-free, lignin-free materials, the boxes resist dust, dirt, and light infiltration yet still allow a slight amount of air circulation. Use acid-free tissue paper or clean cotton cloth as padding.

C) To store small paper mementos, consider mounting them in scrapbooks made of acid-free materials. Make sure fasteners are safe too. Newspaper clippings are inherently acidic, so they become yellow and crumbly with age. If you want to store newspaper articles or announcements as heirlooms, photocopy them onto acid-free paper. Using an off-white paper that resembles newsprint produces the most authentic look.

basic storage components

From simple boxes to elaborate cabinets, great storage solutions take many shapes. This chapter explores your options and explains why certain components excel in specific applications. You'll find useful advice about how to design, build, shop, or even improvise with free materials.

hanging systems

Hooks and pegs are the most basic of storage devices. Close behind are systems that let you store whole collections of things by hanging them across a wall. Because hanging systems are easy to install and relatively inexpensive, they are common in garages and utility rooms. But they are equally effective elsewhere.

Hooks

Everything from coats and hats to ladders and bikes fits on hooks, provided you pick the right size for the task. Hooks with a substantial upward curve hold things better than straighter hooks.

Though you can attach hooks to walls or other surfaces individually, it often makes sense to screw several to a backer board and then attach that to a wall. Besides creating a more unified look, this allows you to space the hooks where you want without worrying about making a secure connection to drywall at each location. Attach the backer to wall studs with 3-inch screws.

DECORATIVE OVER-THE-DOOR HOOK

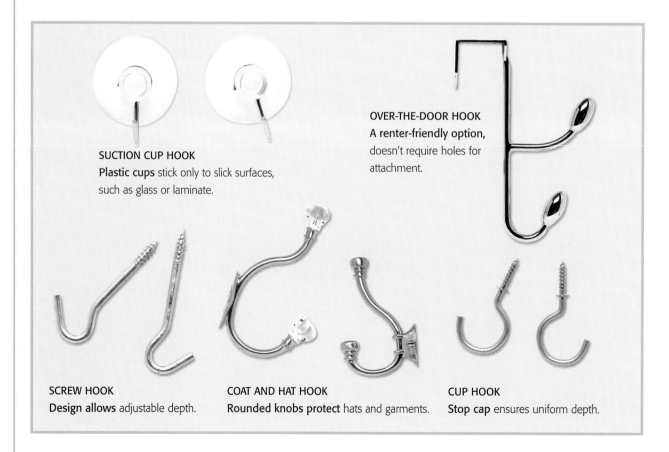

SUCTION CUP HOOK
Plastic cups stick only to slick surfaces, such as glass or laminate.

OVER-THE-DOOR HOOK
A renter-friendly option, doesn't require holes for attachment.

SCREW HOOK
Design allows adjustable depth.

COAT AND HAT HOOK
Rounded knobs protect hats and garments.

CUP HOOK
Stop cap ensures uniform depth.

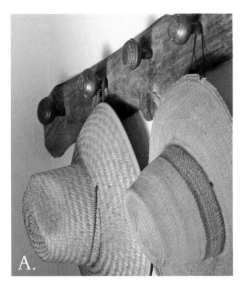

A.

B.

C.

D.

A) Old brass doorknobs make great pegs for hanging hats or jackets.

B) Cubbies in this mudroom are equipped with hooks rather than hangers on a rod for a simple reason: Children far prefer the simplicity of hooks.

C) Shaker pegs create a simple and effective coat rack in this entry.

D) A hanging rail system keeps tools within reach above the kitchen sink.

Pegboard

Your dad probably had pegboard in his garage, and maybe you do too. But that's not the only place where perforated hardboard can be used. Julia Child put it up in her kitchen after first painting the board with outlines of her pots so that she'd know where to put them back. For a retro look, you could do the same. You could also use it to line the walls of utility closets or the backs of cupboard doors—wherever you need to hang things and want the ability to easily rearrange or add to the collection.

Besides standard pegboard made from wood scraps, you can now find pegboard made of steel. The metal is more durable, and hooks stay put much better. However, it costs more and is not as widely available (see Resources, pages 188–189).

Home centers and lumberyards almost always have standard pegboard in stock. Don't waste your time on ⅛-inch-thick board. Buy the ¼-inch-thick type, which is much less likely to buckle or tear. If you don't like the natural brown color, paint the board before you install it.

Grid Systems

Metal grid systems started out as a display solution for retail stores. They do everything that pegboard does, and more, because the metal is stronger and accessories grip better. Plus, grids have a more upscale look, so you might prefer them in a room such as a kitchen.

Like pegboard, grid systems need to protrude slightly from the wall so accessories fasten correctly. Manufacturers sell brackets that create this gap.

Slotwall

This kind of system, also called slatwall, also began as an option for retail stores. In homes, slotwall is found mostly in garages, mudrooms, and closets, though you can use it in other rooms as well.

The basic component is a panel with rows of parallel, horizontal slots. In most residential systems, the panels are made of PVC or CVPC, a related plastic. Most store displays use panels made of MDF, a wood-fiber product.

If you wish to use the slotwall concept and slotwall accessories in your home but don't want any of these materials in your main living spaces, you can duplicate the function by installing parallel rows of solid hardwood backed by spacers.

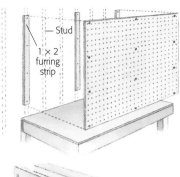

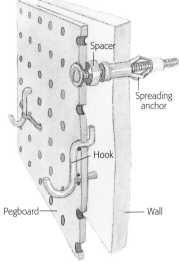

The trick with pegboard is to leave a space behind it so the hooks can slip in. Create this gap with furring strips or with spacers on screws. Furring creates a neater edge and a firmer surface. Spacers are easier to install.

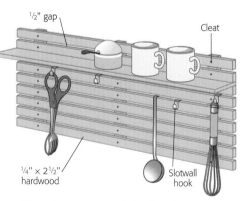

To make your own slotwall system, screw hardwood slats to cleats at least ½ inch thick. This offset lets you insert the hooks.

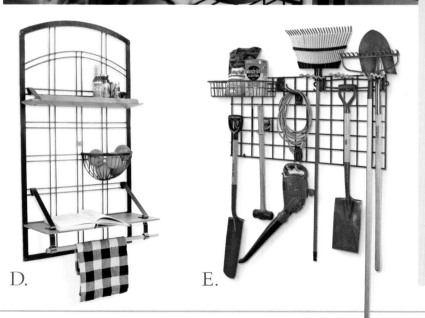

A.

B.

C.

D.

E.

A) Inexpensive and easy to find, standard pegboard has been a fixture of home workshops for decades.

B) Metal pegboard holes don't crumble over time, as holes in standard pegboard often do. This means that hooks are much less likely to wobble or fall out of the metal material. The type of metal pegboard shown here has vertical slots rather than holes, so you need slot-type accessories.

C) Companies sell slotwall with slats in different sizes. Most accessories fit slats spaced 3 inches on center, the standard dimension of slotwall used in stores.

D) Custom grids add decorative appeal but don't have as many accessories as standard 2-inch grid openings do.

E) Many types of hangers are available for grid systems, so you can probably find one that works with almost any hand tool or piece of sports gear you need to store.

shelves

Nothing provides as much storage space as inexpensively and simply as basic shelves. But shelves can also go far beyond basic. If you embellish them with molding, they take on the appearance of fine furniture. If you add vertical dividers, they become cubbyholes. Outfit them with baskets or bins and they become almost as useful for hiding things as cabinets are. This chameleon quality allows you to use shelving throughout the house to store and display a wide array of materials, from books and collectibles to stereo gear and tools.

These shelves have several features that help make the room seem bigger and more open. The upper shelves float on hidden supports, creating an airy look. And the entire unit is recessed into the wall, which makes the room seem less crowded because there is more floor space for other uses.

Design Considerations

The bigger a shelving unit and its components, the more the piece will affect the look of the room it's in. Keep this in mind as you decide whether to get thick, solid shelves or ones made of lighter-looking materials, such as wire or glass. Appearance may matter less in a garage or a pantry than it does in a living room or a bedroom.

You can mount individual shelves on brackets or add them to cabinets or furniture. If you want an entire system, though, one of your first decisions will be whether to design built-in shelving or buy a modular system that comes as a kit or in components.

Built-in. Built-in shelving becomes part of a house and adds to its architectural appeal. Because the shelves are designed for a specific space, they allow you to use every available inch. Options range from simple shelves fitted into a niche to elaborate bookcases trimmed with molding. In some places, you can save floor space by recessing the shelving at least partway into a wall.

Modular. Modular shelving provides an almost instant storage solution. Though it's possible to build modular units from scratch, most people buy kits or components at a store, take them home, and put the pieces together. This usually requires just a few tools and a few hours. If you move, you can take this type of shelving with you.

Heights and Depths

Unless you want to use a ladder or a stepstool, follow the height guidelines on pages 12–13. Basically, keep the top shelf no higher than 72 inches if you want most adults to be able to reach it easily. To allow room for things to sit on that shelf, the top of a bookcase or wall system should be at least a foot higher.

Choose a shelf depth appropriate for what you will store. Common sizes range from 5½ to 24 inches. Over countertops, shelves are usually 12 inches deep, sometimes 16. Under countertops, they are deeper in order to take advantage of the available space. In kitchens, counters are typically 24 inches deep, so shelves underneath tend to be almost as deep.

Shelves near the floor are ideal for children, but adults have a hard time reaching to the back if the shelves are deep and low. Consider replacing the lowest shelf with a drawer, or improvise by placing items in a basket or box that you can pull out when you need something inside.

With custom touches, shelving becomes an important part of a room's appeal. This unit began as a very basic bookcase. It was transformed with wheels and back panels made of different colors of cloth glued to sheets of foam-core board. Hook-and-loop dots (inset) were used to attach the panel, so it's easy to remove and re-cover if the room's décor changes.

Most shelves exist in a world of right angles, but there are other options, as this built-in bookshelf shows.

Keeping Shelves from Sagging

At first glance, a bookcase made of real maple or oak doesn't appear all that different from one made of particleboard coated to look like maple or oak. But load up the shelves with heavy books and look again. If the bookcase is 3 feet wide, the solid boards will probably stay straight, while the particleboard shelves will almost certainly sag over time. To stay straight, the particleboard shelves would need to be in a skinnier bookcase or one with a center support. Understanding how the materials compare helps you buy or build shelves that will work well for years.

How long can a shelf be? The total length doesn't matter, just the distance between supports. The chart below shows the maximum distance that will keep shelves from sagging more than ⅛ inch over 45 inches. It assumes that items on the shelves weigh up to 40 pounds per square foot.

There are many creative ways to build shelves. If you leave some ends unsupported, as this design does, keep spans shorter than usual.

PUSHING THE LIMIT

If spans in the chart (below left) don't fit what you have in mind for a design, there are various ways to create longer ones and still avoid sagging. You can also use these strategies to fix sagging shelves.

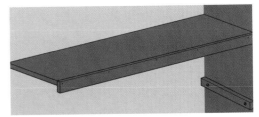

Attach a wooden cleat to the front or back of the shelf, or both.

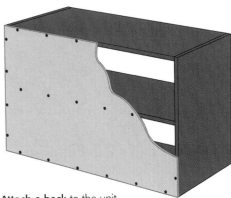

Attach a back to the unit, and fasten it to the shelves.

Maximum Shelf Spans

| Type of material | When shelf thickness is | | | |
	5/8"	3/4"	1"	1¾"
	maximum shelf span between supports is:			
Oak or maple		36"	49"	85"
Plywood	29"	34"	46"	
Cherry or poplar		34"	45"	79"
Soft pine		33"	44"	76"
Medium-density fiberboard (MDF)	18"	21"	28"	
Particleboard	16"	19"	25"	

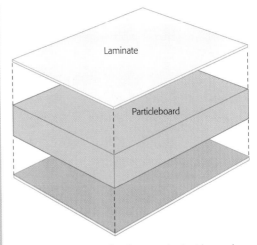

Glue high-pressure laminate to both sides and one edge of particleboard. Laminate the edge after you do the sides. (Melamine, a different kind of plastic coating, does not add significant stiffness.)

Choosing Shelf Boards

Inexpensive pine boards with knots make good shelves. But check the curved lines on the ends. Boards with a dark spot surrounded by circular lines are likely to split. Boards with curved lines that extend across most of the board will cup in the direction opposite to how the lines curve. This happens because the lines, which show the tree's annual growth layers, tend to straighten out as the wood dries.

■ **For shelves.** Place the curves of the growth layers down so the "cup" will face up (see top right illustration). Otherwise, a hump will form at the center of the shelf, causing things to wobble.

■ **Top of a bookcase.** Place the lines curving up. This keeps the joint with the sides tight at the front, where it's most noticeable.

Supporting Adjustable Shelves

There are many ways to support adjustable shelves. Here are some of the most popular methods.

■ **Shelf pins.** These small metal or plastic pieces fit into holes on the sides of the bookcase or cabinet, and the shelves rest on them. Be careful to match the shelf pins' diameter to the size of the holes. Some support pins are a metric size (often 5 mm), while others are ¼ inch. If you expect to move shelves frequently, or if shelf pins on your existing storage units have become wobbly, consider using supports with matching metal sleeves.

■ **Metal standards.** These narrow pieces have slots that hold little clips, which support the shelves. If you build or buy shelving with this type of support system, go for recessed standards, which fit into a groove cut into the sides of the shelves. It's possible to nail standards onto the sides without first cutting a recess, but this causes bulging. You then need to shorten the shelves, leaving gaps on the ends, or cut two small bites out of each end of the shelves.

■ **Wooden standards.** This system, which you can build from thin strips of wood, is often found in kitchen cabinets from the early 1900s. It works best where there is a face frame to tuck the strips behind. Nail, screw, or glue the notched uprights into place and move the horizontal supports to adjust the shelves.

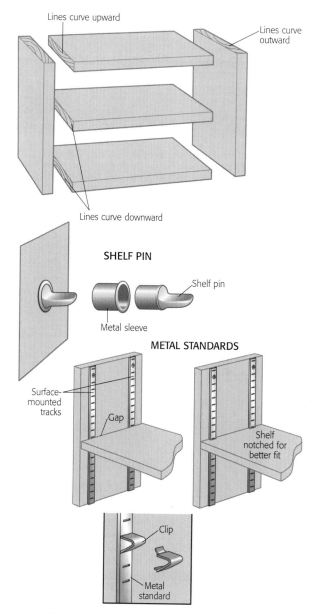

Lines curve upward

Lines curve outward

Lines curve downward

SHELF PIN

Shelf pin

Metal sleeve

METAL STANDARDS

Surface-mounted tracks

Gap

Shelf notched for better fit

Clip

Metal standard

WOODEN STANDARDS

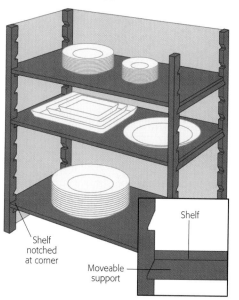

Shelf notched at corner

Shelf

Moveable support

Creating Simple Bracket Shelves

The simplest bracket shelves are nothing more than metal supports with a board on top. From there, though, they get more interesting. You can use wooden brackets cut in an intricate shape. Or, instead of a single shelf, you can install a whole wall of them, creating a look similar to that of a built-in bookcase.

Bracket shelves stand in for a tall bookcase in this child's room.

A bracket shelf with pegs attached to a board underneath provides a place to hang hats, towels, and clothes. This type of shelf is often used in nurseries as a place to showcase special toys, pictures, and birth announcements. Favorite outfits can be hung below to decorate the room once the clothes have been grown out of.

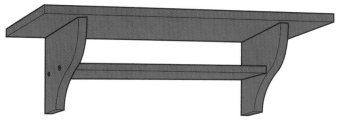

This is a satisfying project for even a beginning woodworker, and you can adapt the design to serve other purposes. For example, you could eliminate the lower shelf and substitute a backboard (as shown in the picture to the left) and add hooks to store keys in an entry. For a bathroom, add a dowel underneath to create a towel bar. Attach keyhole hangers on the back so you can hang this on screws fastened to drywall anchors.

Brackets and shelves trimmed with molding give a Country French flair to this kitchen. Because the brackets are thick, the installer screwed directly through them and into studs. Plugs cover the screw holes.

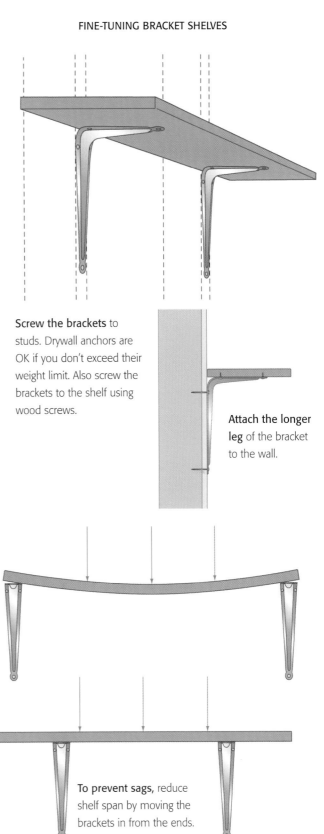

Screw the brackets to studs. Drywall anchors are OK if you don't exceed their weight limit. Also screw the brackets to the shelf using wood screws.

Attach the longer leg of the bracket to the wall.

To prevent sags, reduce shelf span by moving the brackets in from the ends.

Use angle-iron brackets to hang recycling bins on the wall. Bolt the metal brackets into wall studs to give them the support needed to hold up heavy bins. Reinforcing the brackets with diagonal braces will also help them hold up more weight.

Designing Closet or Alcove Shelves

With only a few tools and basic wood-working skills, you can add shelves that solve storage problems in closets and other spaces. Choose solid wood, plywood, or particleboard, depending on your budget and the look you want. Add molding to the front edge for a dressier look.

How to fit shelves. To get a tight fit between shelves and the wall, don't assume the corners of the walls are square. Instead, cut each shelf a little oversize and scribe it to the wall.

1 Determine the distance at the front and back with a folding rule.

2 Usually, you can just cut the shelf to whatever distance is longer, plus 1 inch. But check corners first with a framing square. If both sides angle toward the same side, the longest dimension isn't enough. Add both gaps shown in the illustration, plus 1 inch.

3 Tip the shelf to scribe one end. Cut along the line.

4 Mark the front or back length (whichever is longer) on the other end of the board. Set the compass to the distance from that mark to the end of the board. Trim the board at the scribe line.

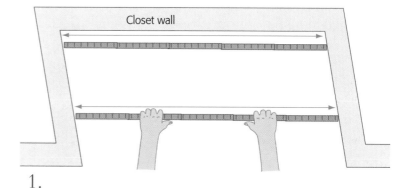

Closet wall

1.

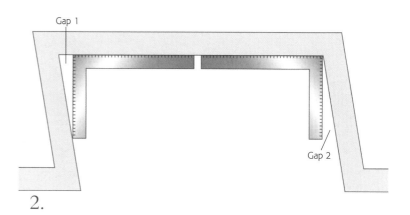

Gap 1

Gap 2

2.

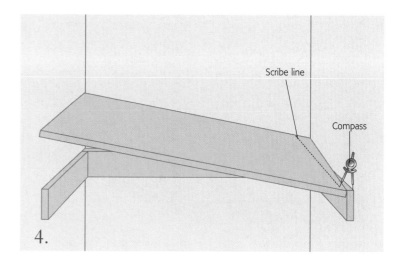

Scribe line

Compass

4.

Designing Hanging Shelves

Hanging shelves can go alongside walls or be suspended over cabinets in the center of a room, where they help divide space without completely closing off either side.

Although hanging shelves may look lightweight, they still need to carry standard loads. You must screw or bolt the supports to framing lumber within the ceiling; you can't just fasten them to drywall. If a joist isn't located in a convenient place, go into the attic or cut through the drywall so you can install 2-by-4 blocking between joists. Fasten into that.

Along a wall, you can use flexible materials, such as rope or cable, as the support structure. But in the center of a room, suspend shelves from rigid materials, such as wood or threaded rod.

Hanging shelves and a cabinet provide needed storage space in this kitchen but don't cut the cook off from conversations going on in the family room just beyond.

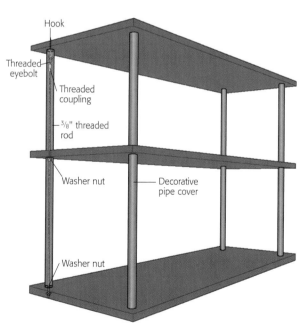

This design works especially well in places where you need storage but don't want to cut off a view into an adjoining room. One or more shelves hang from threaded rods fastened to ceiling joists. You can leave the working parts exposed or hide them by slipping lengths of pipe over the rods and fasteners.

ROPE-HUNG SHELVES

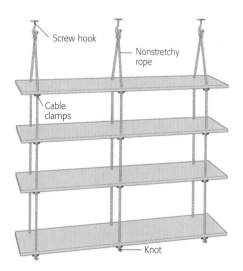

These easy shelves have an airy look because the vertical supports are just ropes. Though it's possible to support the shelves entirely with knots, it's difficult to tie them at precise points. Cable clamps are easy to place precisely. Knot the bottom of each rope and use cable clamps under shelves.

Designing Simple Wall-Hung and Freestanding Shelves

Use these shelves throughout a house: in a kitchen to store dishes, in an office to store supplies, or in a garage to store tools.

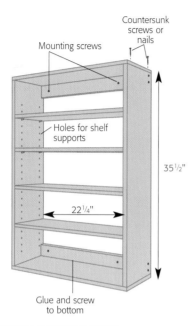

Countersunk screws or nails

Mounting screws

Holes for shelf supports

35½"

22¼"

Glue and screw to bottom

BASIC HANGING SHELVES

This is essentially a box plus a few shelves. If you go by the dimensions shown here, you need just two 10-foot-long boards, plus a few supplies: glue, screws or finishing nails, and shelf support pins. If you need more shelf space, build several units and screw them together.

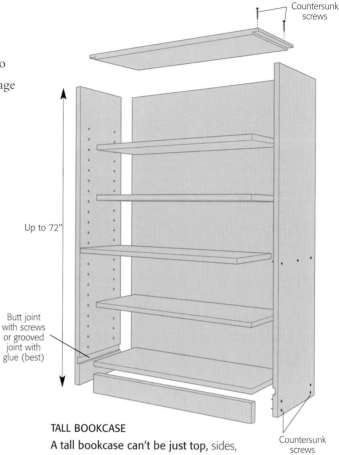

Countersunk screws

Up to 72"

Butt joint with screws or grooved joint with glue (best)

Countersunk screws

TALL BOOKCASE

A tall bookcase can't be just top, sides, and moveable shelves, or it is likely to become an out-of-square parallelogram. For rigidity, this design includes one fixed shelf and a plywood back. It's best to set the back panel into a groove cut into the sides, top, and bottom, but you can just nail the panel into place instead.

3 WAYS TO ADD A BACK PANEL

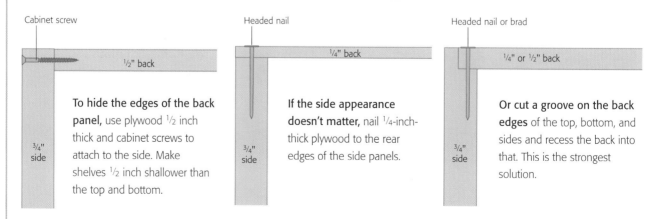

Cabinet screw

½" back

¾" side

To hide the edges of the back panel, use plywood ½ inch thick and cabinet screws to attach to the side. Make shelves ½ inch shallower than the top and bottom.

Headed nail

¼" back

¾" side

If the side appearance doesn't matter, nail ¼-inch-thick plywood to the rear edges of the side panels.

Headed nail or brad

¼" or ½" back

¾" side

Or cut a groove on the back edges of the top, bottom, and sides and recess the back into that. This is the strongest solution.

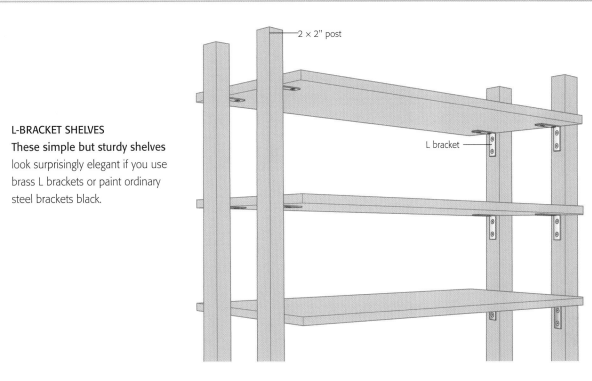

L-BRACKET SHELVES

These simple but sturdy shelves look surprisingly elegant if you use brass L brackets or paint ordinary steel brackets black.

2 × 2" post

L bracket

$1^3/_8$" closet rod

Dowel (see inset)

Center hole $1^3/_4$" from edge

V-groove block keeps dowel from revolving

$^3/_8$" × 2" hardwood dowel

POLE SHELVES

This unit has a nice retro look and is easy to disassemble if you move. It consists of just three materials: shelves, closet rods for vertical pieces, and short lengths of hardwood dowel. Because there is no back or diagonal bracing, you'll need to keep the total height less than 48 inches. Use standard shelf boards or 2-inch-thick planks in your preferred length and width.

The most difficult part is holding the closet rods steady as you drill holes for the short dowels that support the shelves. Use a drill press or a homemade V-groove block. When you drill holes in the shelves, use a spade or Forstner bit or a hole saw slightly wider than the closet rods.

Shopping for Ready-Made Shelves

If you don't want to build your own shelves, choose from many ready-made systems. Modular designs allow you to mix and match components. Try to buy enough components for future needs, as parts from other manufacturers might not fit.

Standards and brackets. Probably the most common kind of instant shelving, these systems have metal brackets that fit into slotted strips known as standards, which are screwed to the wall (see page 51). You add shelves of wood, particleboard, or wire. Some types are sturdier or easier to install than others.

■ **Twin-pin brackets.** These fit into standards with pairs of slots, carry more weight, and are less prone to wobbling than systems with single slots. Brackets also differ in how they keep shelves from sliding off. Some have an integrated lip, while others require you to attach the shelves with screws or adhesive pads.

■ **Hanging systems.** Standards that clip over a top rail are easier to install than independent standards. But check the specifics. If the only attachment to the wall is at the top rail, the system probably has a lower weight limit than one that features each standard also fastened to studs.

Freestanding wire shelving. This type is very strong and is popular in kitchens and pantries styled after commercial kitchens, where identical shelving is often used. Chrome-plated steel is most common, but you can also find other finishes. Check weight limits before you buy, as manufacturers now produce similar-looking products that may not have the strength of the original type.

Modular wooden shelving. These systems usually have preassembled uprights and shelf boards made from solid wood (generally small pieces glued together). Some manufacturers sell all parts individually, while others sell complete kits. Be sure that any kit you buy has enough shelves to meet your needs. Some manufacturers keep their costs low by selling kits with only a few shelves that are widely spaced.

Helpful Hint

If you choose wire shelving, match the type to your needs. Pantry shelves have closely spaced wires and support heavier loads than similar-looking wire shelves sold for clothes and linen closets. Closer spacing helps keep skinny containers from tipping over, so you might want pantry shelving in other rooms, such as bathrooms, where you store toiletries.

The Floating-Shelf Look

You can dress up wooden shelves supported by brackets and standards so that the shelves appear to float. Buy or paint standards to match the wall. To hide the brackets, nail or glue on a 1-by-3-inch wooden strip along each exposed shelf edge. Make its narrow edge flush with the top of the shelf.

The upper levels of these faux floating shelves are made with 1-by-11 pine boards. The bottom shelf, which is longer and might be used as a seat, is 1-by-12 red oak. It has right-angle wall brackets underneath for extra support.

A.

B.

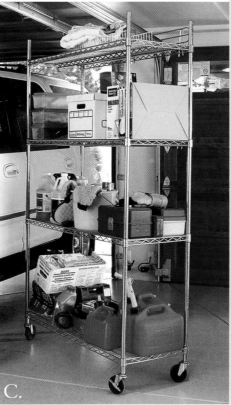

C.

A) A bracket-and-standard shelving system provides plenty of organized storage in this closet. With some systems, you can order special fittings, such as the hangers for the ironing board and vacuum accessories. These standards hang from a top rail and have pairs of slots for twin-pin brackets.

B) Wooden modular systems usually include uprights and shelf boards in different widths and depths. These options give you the flexibility to create everything from simple bookcases to desks.

C) Besides being attractive enough for a kitchen or pantry, chrome-plated wire shelving is a good choice for garages or basements that are occasionally damp. The metal won't mildew or rot, and the chrome coating resists rust. The open design allows air to circulate around stored items.

cabinets

Most people associate cabinets with rows of matching doors and drawers across the walls of a kitchen. While many cabinets do fit this stereotype, modern cabinets can also look like furniture, and they don't necessarily match. In a single room, some cabinets might have glass doors, while others may have wooden doors or maybe none at all. Cabinets aren't just for kitchens either. Garages, bathrooms, dens, family rooms, laundry rooms, even bedrooms or home offices—it's hard to think of places that wouldn't benefit from the easily accessible, attractive storage opportunities that cabinets provide.

Showroom choices. Through a kitchen and bath showroom, a lumberyard, or a home center, you can order factory-made cabinets in three grades:

■ **Stock cabinets.** These mass-produced models cost the least and come in set sizes that vary in increments of 3 inches. You can buy them already assembled or as parts that are cut and finished but not yet put together. By assembling them yourself, you save money.

■ **Semicustom cabinets.** You can have these built to order, but your order has to fit within the manufacturer's basic line. They offer more variety in door design and finishes.

■ **Custom cabinets.** You should be able to get whatever sizes and options you want. However, be aware that many large manufacturers "customize" standard sizes by using spacers and trim rather than designing the cabinets to make every inch count.

Other options. Local woodworkers and small shops make cabinets. They are the best way to go if you want to include special details that you or an architect designs, or if you want new cabinets that match period pieces already in your home. It's also a great option if you want to support local crafts people.

You can also buy components and assemble them to produce finished cabinets, sometimes at a considerable savings. If you're handy, you might decide to build the cabinet boxes and shelves but buy doors and drawers from a company that specializes in making them (see Resources, pages 188–189). Some suppliers deal only with contractors or require large orders, while others are happy to sell one maple dovetail drawer if that's all you need. You'll also have to choose, order, and install the hardware, or hire someone to do this for you. Some small remodeling companies specialize in installing cabinets but don't actually build them.

A.

B.

A) When you order custom cabinets from a local woodworker, you can get details tuned to your personal style, such as a file drawer built into the window seat where you pay bills.

B) Southern colonial plantations inspired the details of the cabinets in this combination living room, library, and media room. But they have a decidedly modern twist. The fluted columns on each side of the TV are actually pullout media storage towers.

C) Cabinets in this kitchen provide loads of storage and function as room dividers, making the eating area more intimate. The combination of translucent and solid doors adds variety and helps the cabinets look both traditional and hip—not always an easy combination to pull off.

C.

Cabinets 101

Essentially, cabinets are big boxes outfitted with shelves, drawers, and maybe doors.

Beyond these basics, you have a great number of choices. It's easy to focus on exterior details, such as the style, finish, and trim. However, the actual storage goes on inside. How that space is organized plays a huge role in determining how useful the cabinets are.

Face frame or frameless? As far as the actual construction goes, cabinets come in two broad categories: framed and frameless.

Framed cabinets, which are more traditional, have a wooden framework about ¾ inch thick that covers the front of the cabinet box. The hinges often show on the front of the doors, but when the doors are open, the hinges are out of the way. There are also face frame cabinets with hinges that can't be seen when the doors are closed.

In frameless cabinets, also known as "European style," the front of the cabinet box is also the front of the cabinet. So when you open the door, the cabinet extends straight back, as there is no lip from a frame. The hinges are completely hidden when the doors are closed but jut into the space when the doors are open.

If you plan to outfit your cabinets mostly with shelves, either style will yield about the same amount of storage. If you're considering numerous drawers, however, frameless cabinets will make better use of your space because they allow for wider drawers. If you want sliding shelves, you'll have slight complications either way because the face frame and the large European hinges both intrude into the opening.

Materials. Most residential cabinets are made of wood or wood-based materials, including plywood, particleboard, and medium-density fiberboard (MDF). Over particleboard, there is often a thin layer of polyvinyl chloride (PVC) printed with a picture of wood. Most closet systems and some kitchen cabinets are made this way. It's not always easy for an untrained eye to see the difference between solid wood and the coated particleboard, but there is a big difference in strength, durability, and odor. To make sure you know what you're buying, inspect the back edge of a shelf, which is usually left uncoated. Or see whether a shelf's wood grain is consistent on the surface and on the edges.

Sizes. Most cabinets are sized in 3-inch increments. The most popular widths are 18, 24, and 30 inches. Some cabinets are just 6 inches across—perfect for a spice rack—while others are as wide as 48 inches.

This living room cabinet has the traditional look of framed construction. One face frame surrounds the upper portion, and another links the drawers and doors on the bottom. The hinges, also traditional, show on the front when the doors are closed but are barely noticeable when the doors are open.

Outfitted with vertical shelf dividers for storing trays, this cabinet is a frameless type. It has European-style hinges, which don't show when the door is closed but project into the cabinet space when the door is open.

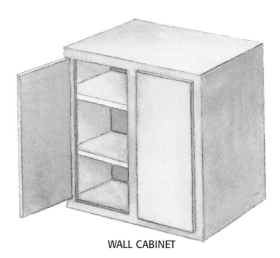

WALL CABINET

■ **Wall cabinets.** Heights vary from 12 to 42 inches, so you can use them in rooms of different heights and in different ways. Most wall cabinets are 12 to 13 inches deep, while cabinets designed to go over a refrigerator can be up to 24 inches deep—making them also just right to use under a window seat.

■ **Base cabinets.** Designed to go under a kitchen countertop, these are usually 34½ inches high and 24 inches deep. Vanity base cabinets are a bit shorter, at 33½ inches, and cabinets built to support desktops are shorter yet, at 29 inches. If you want a variety of counter heights in a kitchen, order a few cabinets sized for other rooms.

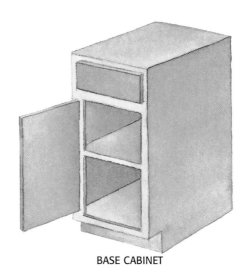

BASE CABINET

■ **Tall cabinets.** Tall usually means 84, 90, or 96 inches high; 9 to 36 inches wide; and 12 to 24 inches deep. Use tall cabinets to house wall ovens or as broom closets, pantries, or storage for a home office or crafts room. They also make good room dividers.

> **Helpful Hint**
>
> If you are trying to re-create the look of cabinets from the early 1900s, think carefully about whether you want a toe-kick (an indented area across the bottom of base cabinets). Toe-kicks allow you to stand close to a countertop without bumping your toes, but vintage cabinets didn't have them. Watch for other details too. Old-time cabinetmakers used face frames, and they installed hinges visible on the front.

TALL CABINET

drawers

When you need storage space that holds a lot and lets you get to it easily, drawers usually do it best. Most cabinet companies build a basic box for the drawer, then screw on a second front piece that matches the style of the cabinet. This allows the same box to be used for dozens of cabinet styles.

Dovetails. When most drawers slid on wooden runners, cabinetmakers learned that the interlocking design of dovetail joints kept drawers intact. Today, dovetail joints aren't as essential because the actual weight of the drawer is usually carried by metal slides. Dovetails are beautiful, however, and they are still a mark of quality, provided the drawers are made of solid wood. Some cabinet companies offer dovetail drawers made of vinyl-coated particleboard. These joints are actually weaker than ones made with dowels or even just nails and glue.

One-piece fronts. When customers don't want double-thick drawer fronts, some companies offer to turn the drawers so that the sides become the front and back.

This creates a neat appearance, but it defeats the purpose of the joinery. If you want drawers with only one piece in front, order half-blind dovetails, which don't show on the front, or a lipped front, which has a shoulder milled into the wood.

Selecting the Best Drawer Slides

Some inexpensive drawers simply slide back and forth on fixed runners. They tend to work fine when you try them out at the store. But once you get home and load them up, they're likely to bind. To avoid this, buy drawers that move on slides equipped with wheels or ball bearings. The best slides have a piece that cups over the wheels or bearings to help keep the drawer from slipping sideways.

Weight rating. Check what weight the drawer slides can safely carry. Some kitchen drawers can only carry 18 pounds. While that's fine for silverware, the drawers won't hold up if you use them to store heavier things. Other drawers can carry 100 pounds or more.

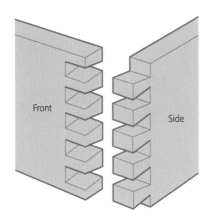

DOVETAIL JOINT
Ends of sides flare toward the front, keeping drawer intact when it is pulled out.

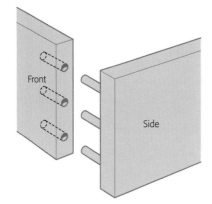

DOWELED JOINT
Dowels go sideways into the front, keeping drawer intact when it is pulled out.

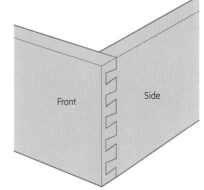

HALF-BLIND DOVETAIL
This is a strong joint, with a neat-looking, single front piece.

Mechanical action. Standard slides extend a drawer only about three-fourths of the way. Full-extension slides, which cost more, have a telescoping mechanism that allows you to get into the very back of the drawers. Standard slides are fine for most purposes, except when you need to pull items straight up from the back of the drawer. Telescoping types help on file drawers and deep drawers where you plan to store tall objects, such as soup pots and small appliances.

Soft-closing mechanisms automatically pull drawers the final few inches. It's a nice touch, but be aware that you will have to pull harder to open the drawer.

The telescoping mechanism on full-extension slides allows the drawer to be pulled all the way out of the cabinet yet remain attached to it.

This drawer has undermount, full-extension slides, so you don't see the hardware and you can reach into the very back of the drawer.

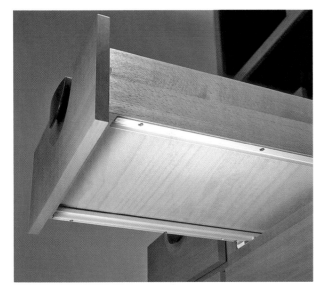

Side-mount slides usually go near the center of a drawer's sides, but these attach at the bottom, creating a neater look.

A decorative panel covers the front of this solid-wood dovetailed drawer.

Sliding Shelves

By converting fixed shelves to sliding shelves, you make them function as drawers, so it's easy to reach what's in the back, even if the shelves are quite deep. But rather than having their own decorative fronts, sliding shelves usually hide behind doors. Because it takes two steps to open a door and pull out a shelf, sliding shelves probably aren't the best choice if you are designing storage from scratch. You'd be better off with drawers. But sliding shelves are ideal retrofits when you want to make existing storage work better. They cost less too, and you can adjust their height if your needs change. Manufacturers offer many types of sliding shelves. The sides may be wood, wire, or metal, and the glides may be mounted at the center or on the sides.

A.

Hybrid Shelves

There are a couple of other ways to design shelves so that they move toward you, as drawers do.

Swing-out shelves pivot out from a cabinet. Over a wide base cabinet, this could make it easier to reach what's inside. Or you could use a narrow swing-out shelf at the front of a cabinet where you store tall items toward the back of the shelf below.

Pull-down shelves have a hinge mechanism that allows you to lower them to a comfortable height. Once you've gotten what you want, a piston gently raises the shelf back into position. Pull-down shelves allow you to make better use of high storage areas, such as the space over a refrigerator. Convenience comes at a price, though. The hardware may cost several hundred dollars per pair.

B.

When you need one drawer to be deeper than another but want them to look equally high, consider the solution shown here: sliding shelves behind a partly false drawer front.

C.

D.

E.

F.

A) Independent sliding shelves move separately and can be set at desired heights.

B) With tandem shelves, everything slides out at once. Glides are on the top and bottom.

C) The door-linked shelf on the bottom pulls out automatically with the door front. The upper shelf is independent.

D) Although slide-out shelves are usually hidden behind cabinet doors, they can still transcend the ordinary. Plain or decorative, sides keep items from slipping off.

E) Pull-down shelves can be lowered to a convenient height. They are especially useful in high cabinets and in houses where someone uses a wheelchair.

F) Swing-out shelves bring the contents out of a cabinet so they are easy to reach.

boxes and bins

oxes and bins corral small items so you can store them efficiently and attractively on shelves, in closets, or simply in stacks on the floor. Having small items in one container reduces visual clutter and makes it much easier to find what you want.

Boxes and bins also help when shelves are very high or very low. Instead of tiptoeing on a ladder or crouching as you look for the item you need, you can pull out the box, move it to a comfortable height, and then look.

■ **Capacity.** For maximum storage space, select boxes or baskets that are rectangular rather than round or tapered. A cube 18 inches across occupies about the same shelf space as a drum that's the same height and diameter, but the cube holds 28 percent more. If that cube had walls that tapered inward by 4 inches from top to bottom, its storage capacity would shrink by almost 10 percent.

■ **Closure.** Some boxes snap shut or latch, while others merely close. Snap-on lids seal out moisture and pests, but they aren't very forgiving if you overload the box. Latches tend to work even when the box is a little overfull. For toy boxes and other containers that don't need to be sealed but do need easy access, choose a box with a lid that just settles into place, or get a bin instead.

■ **Clear or opaque?** Clear storage containers allow you to see what's inside, so you spend less time searching for things and aren't as likely to forget what you have. Opaque containers are better if you want to keep out light, perhaps to prevent fading, or if you don't want your stored items on view.

■ **Ventilation.** For some kinds of storage, you want a watertight, airtight container. But if you are storing dirty laundry until washday, a well-ventilated container works better.

A.

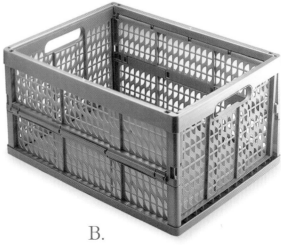

B.

C.

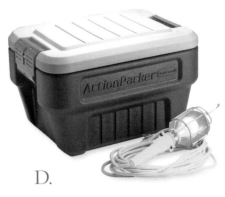

D.

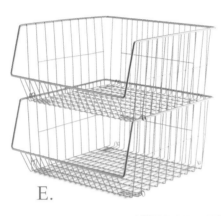

E.

A) Baskets are so attractive that some cabinet companies offer them as an alternative to drawers. These baskets are set into wooden trays that slide on runners, easing strain on the baskets.

B) This plastic crate folds flat, so it's great for temporary storage or for getting things to and from a picnic. It has straight sides, providing more storage space than tapered containers do. And because it's ventilated, the crate is ideal for items that need to air out, such as sports gear.

C) Rectangular baskets without a wooden surround make more efficient use of space, provided their size is a good match for the opening in the cabinet.

D) If you want a container to stay shut even if it's a bit overloaded, look for a latching mechanism, not just a snap-on lid.

E) With their scooped-out shape in front, bins are designed so that you can put things in and take them out easily. They can store everything from socks to recyclables.

F) Lightweight baskets that are easy to carry make great storage containers for children's toys, especially when you keep the baskets where kids can reach them.

F.

Plastic Storage Containers

It's easy to understand why plastic containers are so popular. They're inexpensive, lightweight, readily available, and they hold a lot. If you get clear containers, you can see what you've stored. You can also stack them or keep them on shelves efficiently.

Plastic storage containers don't absorb moisture so they can't rot. That's a good thing except when you go to get rid of them. Plastic boxes that aren't recycled wind up in landfills, where they stay for decades. Try to select containers that you can use for years.

Many plastic containers are marked with a resin code—a number ranging from 1 through 7 inside a three-arrow recycling symbol. Containers with this mark are easier to recycle. Numbers 1 through 6 are specific plastics, so recycling programs are more likely to have a market for them. The number 7 is a mixture of plastics, which makes recycling more difficult. Over time, some types of plastic release chemicals that damage certain stored items. For a discussion about this, see page 40.

If you expect that your containers will be empty part of the time, look for a design that allows you to store them efficiently. The containers at left nest inside each other.

If you plan to stack boxes once they're loaded, check whether their lids and bases fit together well (below). Most containers with domed lids can't be stacked.

With their handles flipped, the same baskets shown above stack for use as bins.

Thrifty Alternatives

American companies spend more than $90 billion a year on packaging materials. With a little creativity, and without spending a dime, you can reuse their containers to meet your own storage needs. Stores that sell packaged food in bulk are a particularly good source.

Bin-type boxes. These have handy cutouts that allow you to see and reach what's stored inside. They're perfect for helping you organize everything from mittens and hats to packages of soup mix. You can use the boxes as they are or you can paint the exteriors so you don't have to stare at labels for peas or pasta. Standard water-based wall paint works fine, but the water in it sometimes curls the cardboard slightly. To avoid this, use a shellac-based primer first.

Clear plastic containers. Often used for salad mixes and prepared deli foods, clear plastic containers are generally made of a type of polyester known as polyethylene terephthalate, or PET. This plastic, which carries the number 1 in the plastic recycling symbol, is one of the kinds that professional conservators use to store heirlooms. Because the plastic is clear and inert, the containers are ideal for storing many things, such as collections of small items and crafts supplies. If the containers seem too flexible, nest two and use them as one stiffer container.

Become a cardboard connoisseur. If you want to stack bin-type boxes, look for containers that have tabs and slots that allow one box to hook into the next. This will keep your pile from toppling.

A collection of shoe boxes can turn simple shelves into a storage cabinet. Depending on how elaborate you want to get, you can add decorative covers, labels, or handles made of rope or ribbon.

Every room in a house benefits from effective storage solutions. This chapter examines each setting, from entries on through kitchens and garages, and discusses the specific challenges presented by the activities that go on there. It shows a range of options so that you can select the ones that best suit your needs.

room-by-room storage solutions

entries

The entries to your house live a double life, and that makes them a challenge. As the first stop in your home, they set the tone for what family members and visitors experience. So you want the entry tidy and welcoming. But spaces just inside the front and back doors also need to be storage areas. They serve as catchalls for shoes and keys, jackets and hats, and maybe junk mail or things that need to be delivered elsewhere the next time you run errands.

With efficient storage space, entries can accommodate all this stuff and still look neat. But if the storage isn't right there and easy to use, clutter is sure to continue. No one, having just shed muddy shoes, is likely to carry them to another room to put them away. If you have kids, you may have discovered that even opening the door to a coat closet may be too much for them to do when they're racing through. Instead, try cubbies equipped with pegs or hooks.

B.

A.

A) Half walls with built-in storage separate this entry from a lower level, allowing light from the windows there to stream into the entry.

B) The lid of one of the half walls lifts up to reveal space for keys, change, and game tickets. There's even a receptacle to charge cell phones.

C) Adding a mirror to an entryway closet lets you give yourself a last quick check as you head out the door. Also consider adding a small shelf or basket for a hairbrush and keys, and hooks for a purse and an umbrella.

D) Cubbies provide ample storage in this entryway. Short cubbies are used for sports equipment, shoes, and backpacks, while taller cubbies equipped with hooks are great for hanging jackets. A bronze bucket provides a place to put wet umbrellas so they don't have to be carried dripping through the house.

E) Easy to use and elegantly simple, a low niche in an entryway wall provides a handy place to store shoes. The nearby bench and broom are other practical features.

F) Thanks to well-planned cabinetry, this wide rear entry does quadruple duty. Besides being a laundry area and a mudroom, it serves as a home message center and a mail-sorting station, with cubbies for each family member above the far end of the counter on the left. An especially nice touch is the low bench, good for folding laundry or taking off shoes.

Front Entries

How you arrange storage space in a front entry has a lot to do with what kind of house you have and how it is oriented on your lot. Some houses have gracious foyers, yet they rarely see any traffic because everyone uses a side or back door, or maybe a door from the garage. Other houses have a front door that opens right into the living room and is in daily use. A small entry that no one uses is no problem. Just ignore it or add decoration if you wish. But other entries benefit from more attention.

Small, busy entries. These are the most challenging. If you ask people to take off their shoes at the door, dealing with the cast-offs is probably your biggest concern. Solutions might include a narrow bench with storage underneath, a stool along with a wall-mounted rack, or even a simple basket. A row of hooks or pegs makes a good stand-in for a coat closet. After you have those essentials, add embellishments, such as a small mirror with a shelf underneath for keys and maybe a hairbrush, or a row of cubbies so you can sort and store mail as you walk in.

Large but little-used entries. These give you an opportunity to add storage that can ease the burden on another room in your house. For example, you might add an armoire and use it to store winter coats, thus freeing space in your bedroom closet. Or you could add a chest and store crafts materials that are now scattered among several rooms. Choose storage units that suit the style of the entry.

Large, busy entries. You can have a lot of fun redoing one of these. There's enough room to indulge in ample storage for coats and shoes, a bench to sit on, a home message center, and more.

A.

B.

A) Discreetly masking its purpose, a shoe cabinet provides storage in tilt-out drawers.

B) In a busy front entry that also needs to look tidy, this dual-purpose cabinet hides a few dozen shoes and boots and allows people to make a quick check on their appearance before they head out the door.

C) Small drawers, mounted on a wall or set on a chest, are a good place to store keys, spare change, and errand notes. You can also use many other types of containers, including baskets on a shelf or pails hung from pegs.

C.

D.

E.

F.

G.

D) Built-in Mission-style cabinets and wainscot paneling create useful storage space and add to the décor of this entry. The rail for the coat hooks is recessed into the paneling, which creates more space on the bench below.

E) If your entry includes a stairway, be sure to include the area underneath in your planning, unless it's already being used for stairs to a basement. The owners of this house tucked in an easily accessible, generously sized shoe rack.

F) Modeled after a Victorian hall tree but with a cushion instead of holes for umbrellas, this unit would be a gracious touch near a door used by guests.

G) These units extend all the way under the stairway and roll out on heavy-duty drawer glides, just as rollout pantry shelves do in a kitchen. The cabinets are outfitted with closet rods and spaces for boots and shoes.

Mudrooms

Virtually all houses used to have mudrooms or at least a back porch. People needed a place to shed their muddy boots and wet coats and to set down firewood. In the 1950s, as it became more common for builders to attach garages to houses, mudrooms fell out of favor. Today they're considered luxuries. People who have them say they would never go back to doing without them.

If your house lacks a room specifically designated as a mudroom, you can use other space near the back door to accomplish some of the same things. You'd want it to have the same amenities as a front entry, but you may need more storage space if most of the family uses it daily.

Replacing part of a wall alongside a stairway, a cabinet converts this entry into a functional mudroom and gives it an artsy style. The low, deep cubbies double as a bench, while smaller sections above provide additional storage.

A) Tucked into a corner near the back door, this compact area provides a bench and storage space for shoes, coats, and hats. There's even a TV for someone doing laundry at the other end of the room.

B) A few pine boards and some Shaker pegs provide abundant storage in this entry, just in from the garage. The builder cut off the sharp corner of the upper storage unit and inserted an angled piece so no one would get poked. Shoes go under the low bench against the wall or under the sturdy table, which doubles as a seat.

C) With six shelves in each vertical section, these mud-room cubbies can be adjusted as children need taller spaces to hang jackets.

D) A wall cabinet alongside basement stairs holds all the necessities for coming and going. Below the dog biscuits, a dog bed tucks into a wide cubby.

living and family rooms

Family gathering spots have different storage needs depending on how they are used. In rooms that are mostly for entertaining, the main challenges may involve protecting and displaying collectibles. In other rooms, storing electronic gear, books, or games may be bigger issues.

Funky storage solutions usually don't belong in these areas, but built-in shelves and well-designed cabinets work nicely. Also consider the many ways to incorporate storage into furniture. If you have a wood-burning fireplace or stove, you'll appreciate storage that helps keep that area tidy.

A.

A) To keep the large television from dominating the relatively small room, the owners set it on a shelf alongside the fireplace rather than over it. Cushions in two sizes fit on shelves above and below.

B) Book-lined walls make dens or living rooms especially cozy. These shelves extend over the doorway, which not only adds storage but also makes this room seem more separate from the adjoining entry. The thick wall signals to visitors that they are entering the family's personal space.

C) Although a stunning view is the main attraction, built-in cabinetry around this window seat also adds to its appeal. The cabinets provide a convenient hiding place for oversized games or crafts supplies. The cabinet on the left doubles as a backrest, and both it and the cabinet on the right serve as safe landings for cups.

D) A full wall of cabinets provides a lot of storage in a living room but can seem sterile if you see only closed doors. Incorporating open areas and contrasting colors or textures creates a livelier look.

Hiding the TV

Televisions have changed a lot over the past few years, and so have their storage requirements. The most obvious difference is that many newer models have much bigger screens but far thinner profiles. Some are still heavyweights, but others are so light and slender that you can hang them like pictures on a wall.

The other huge change is in the way television signals are broadcast. Analog is being phased out by digital, high-definition signals. With that shift come several changes that affect how you store your TV. Even if you adapt your old TV to work with the new digital signals, it makes sense to ensure any new storage systems can accommodate newer equipment.

Most of the time, this built-in entertainment center looks like a pleasantly asymmetrical cabinet with a curious cutout in the right panel. But when the owners tire of looking at the television, they can pull the side panels, which are sliding doors, toward the center. The cutout allows the sound system, hidden behind the translucent doors at the bottom, to remain accessible at all times.

Screen shape. Older screens were almost square because analog signals were sent to fit on a screen with a 4–3 ratio of width to height. That meant a screen 24 inches high was always 32 inches wide. The new digital signals fit a wide-screen format with a 16–9 ratio. This makes televisions more horizontal, like movie screens. So under the new format, a screen 24 inches high stretches to 43 inches wide. For someone playing a video game or watching a movie, the wider screen is great because more of the action is in view. But for storage, it means that if you buy a new wide-screen TV, you may not be able to fit it into the cabinet you now use, unless you switch to a shorter TV.

TV depth. Old picture-tube televisions are about 2 feet deep even though their screens are relatively small. While newer sets often have much larger screens, some are quite slender when viewed from the side. This gives you more options for storing them. If you choose a flat-panel model with a plasma or liquid-crystal display, your main decision will be whether to treat it as a piece

of art or hide it in furniture. The depth, usually less than 5 inches, isn't much of an issue. At the other end of the scale are traditional-style TVs based on cathode-ray tubes, which require as much depth as ever. In the middle are rear-projector types with a liquid-crystal display or one of the other new technologies. While too heavy and bulky to mount on a wall, they are slender enough to fit in many bookcases and cabinets. You don't need huge cabinets or armoires for them.

Viewing distance. With an analog signal, you need to store a television quite a ways from where you sit to watch it. Otherwise, you'll see the individual dots that form the picture. Digital signals let you sit closer because they create much finer definition. A screen 30 inches across (measured diagonally, as the industry does) needs to be only 6 feet from you, rather than 8. For larger TVs, add about 2 feet to the minimum viewing distance for each additional 10 inches of screen size.

Wide-screen televisions can fit where older-style cathode-ray tubes could never go, thanks to their thinner profiles. The easier venting requirements of gas or electric fireplaces open up even more possibilities, including placing the TV on top of the fireplace. That puts both of the main attractions of the living room in one place. A sliding door for the TV is nice for when the glow of a fire is all you want.

New TVs and How to Store Them

Type of Television	Depth	Screen Size (Diagonal)	Storage Solutions
LCD TVs	3–5"	Usually 23–45" but can go to 82"	Lightweight enough to hang like a picture, or can go in a cabinet or on a shelf
Plasma TVs	3–5"	Usually 42–60" but can go to 103"	Lightweight enough to hang like a picture, or can go in a cabinet or on a shelf
Rear-projection microdisplays (LCD, DLP, LCoS)	15–19"	47–70"	On shelf or in cabinet that can support 200 pounds or more
Rear-projection HDTVs with cathode-ray tubes	24" or more	47–60"	Deep shelf or cabinet that can support 200 pounds or more
Picture-tube (cathode-ray tube) HDTVs	24" or more	26–36"	Deep shelf or cabinet that can support 200 pounds or more

Storing Audio and Video Gear

Storage needs are changing here too, primarily because many people now want to integrate sound systems with their TVs to create more of a home theater experience. There are also DVRs, DVD players, and cable boxes or satellite receivers to store. And there are still all of the old issues, such as providing enough space and ensuring adequate ventilation so components don't get too hot.

Speaker placement. The new HDTVs allow for six audio channels, but words spoken on the TV still need to come primarily from the same direction as the screen or it will seem odd. Place the main speaker directly above or below the screen (see illustration at right). If that's not possible, point it toward you. Hide speakers behind a fabric screen.

Ventilation. Storage systems must allow a steady airflow to disperse the heat that all audio and video gear generates, or the equipment can be damaged. Avoid stacking components directly on top of each other. Space them, or place them on separate shelves a few inches apart. If you have closed doors over the front of a cabinet, you need vents on the back and possibly louvers between shelves.

Doors. DVD players, CD players, and other components are less than 18 inches wide, so they work fine behind standard doors. Covering a TV is more problematic. Swinging doors take up too much space in the room. Pocket styles work, but only when a cabinet is no more than twice as wide as it is deep; with many wide-screen TVs, the geometry doesn't work out. Sliding doors are fine if there is room on both sides of the TV for them to open. Also consider tambour doors, similar to the covers on old-fashioned rolltop desks, or doors that fold up on special hinges.

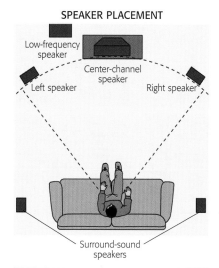

SPEAKER PLACEMENT

Low-frequency speaker

Center-channel speaker

Left speaker

Right speaker

Surround-sound speakers

A.

Full-Screen Movies

If you're tempted to get a big-screen TV only to watch occasional movies, you can save considerable storage space by investing in a front projector, which takes up less than a square foot on a shelf. Be sure to get a projector designed for movies, not business presentations. Plug it into a computer, a DVD player, or a TV tuner. Aim the beam at a pull-down screen, or improvise with a white wall or a sheet. Some projectors are designed to be suspended from a ceiling, or you can set one on a lift-up shelf. Either solution saves you from having to adjust the beam each time. Modern projectors compensate for angles, so they deliver a rectangular image even if the light does not stream in directly from the front.

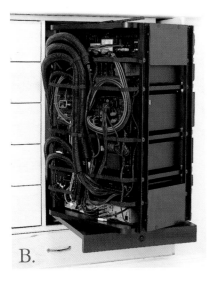

A) To recess equipment into a wall or cabinet, you can buy ready-made shelving that pushes into the wall once you've connected all the wires.

B) This unit swivels, so you can easily reach the back to change wiring.

C) When a TV is mounted over a fireplace, the main speaker should go on top, with auxiliary speakers on the sides. To give this setup a more unified appearance, the owners added CD storage cabinets on each side and inserted panels in the doors that look similar to the speaker covers below.

D) Flat-panel TVs and front projector screens are so thin that you can recess them between bookshelves. In this wall unit, the main speaker, which delivers 80 percent of the sound, is right in the middle, where it belongs. Auxiliary speakers are on the side shelves. Other components fit on slide-out shelves in the base cabinet, which is equipped with louvers at the bottom to let out heat. CDs and related supplies go on the right.

E) Even as TVs have gotten bigger, many sound systems have become smaller. This sleek, modern cabinet leaves the TV within view but frames it with cabinets that have push-to-open latches. An open shelf for the pared-down sound system eliminates the need for an elaborate venting system.

Specialized Storage in Living Rooms

In some living rooms, there's little need for storage because nothing happens there. But in the room where your family does gather, good storage becomes essential. It's the best way to avoid being overwhelmed by magazines, games, and all the other things that become clutter when there's no option for putting them away.

Storing board games. Board games come in boxes, so they should be easy to store. Unfortunately, the sizes aren't consistent. The boxes also break over time. Corral the clutter by consolidating all the pieces into one master game set. Take out the boards and label them near an outside edge. Attach vertical dividers, like those you'd use to hold cookie sheets, so that you can store the game boards on edge in a cabinet. Organize all of the rules and directions in one binder. Put game pieces and play money in plastic bags, then put the bags in a box with enough room left for other game essentials, such as a timer, scratch paper, and pencils. Store the binder and the box next to the game boards.

To keep firewood dry without bringing large quantities inside, establish a covered storage area near the house but outside. This carport setup works beautifully. Built mostly of concrete blocks topped with a concrete countertop, it provides 10½ feet for wood storage plus space for a built-in cabinet.

Storing firewood. Firewood storage is no longer a concern in houses where flames burn on gas or electricity. But it's still an issue in homes with traditional fireplaces or wood-burning stoves. Large amounts of firewood should be kept outdoors, off the ground, and away from the walls of your house. But the wood still must be sheltered from rain and snow. Storing large amounts of firewood inside isn't a good idea because wood releases a lot of moisture when it dries and may harbor termites, carpenter ants, or other pests.

One of the best ways to prevent clutter is to store items as close as possible to the places where you will use them. This window seat is designed to make that easy. Ideal for reading, playing board games, or simply staring at the view outside, it has built-in storage underneath.

Freestanding racks, such as this steel one, work well for small quantities of firewood inside. In a carpeted room, set the rack on a hearth or tiles so debris is easy to clean up.

Storing collectibles. Some people love decorating with collectibles, while others consider them clutter. Whatever camp you're in, there are two basic truths to keep in mind.

First, collectibles do warm up a home and make it look like your personal space rather than a pristine setting in a catalog. If you have stories to tell about how you got the items or what makes each one different, they'll serve as icebreakers when you entertain company.

But the second point is equally true: Collectibles collect dust. How many you store and how you display them can make a huge difference in how much time you need to spend cleaning.

Outfitted with glass shelves, this storage area functions almost as a window, channeling light from the room beyond into the living room. The glass doors on both sides also keep out dust, which is especially noticeable on glass shelves.

Four Ways to Store Magazines

File them in a basket.

Add a shelf to a coffee table.

Store issues you want to keep in labeled holders on shelves.

Sew or buy sofa pockets.

kitchens

Efficient storage matters more in a kitchen than in any other room. Luckily, this was discovered long ago. Clever people have come up with many creative solutions, ranging from better organizing strategies to systems that help you sort and store things efficiently.

If your kitchen doesn't function well but you're not sure why, pinpoint the areas worth attention. Mentally walk through the steps that it takes to prepare a meal and clean up afterward. How many trips back and forth do you make to prepare a salad? Are the spinner, knife, cutting board, bowl, and salad servers each in a different direction? What about the items you need to prepare breakfast? The answers will help you zero in on specific storage issues that are worth solving.

Kitchen Storage Strategies

■ **Purge.** Get rid of things you never use.

■ **Save steps.** Store items you do use as close as possible to where you need them. Keep glasses and plates by the dishwasher. If that won't work, put them by the table. Pots and pans, wooden spoons and spatulas, and cooking oil should go by the range or cooktop.

■ **Make it easy.** Place the things you use every day where they are easy to reach. Use very high or very low spaces for things like holiday serving pieces.

■ **Consolidate.** Group items that you use together, such as baking supplies or things you use while preparing school lunches.

■ **Rearrange.** If space is short, move light bulbs and other household supplies to another room. Also consider moving bulk food to a pantry closet or an armoire in a nearby room. Parcel bulk food into smaller containers that you keep in the kitchen.

Limiting storage to base cabinets makes a kitchen seem brighter and more spacious, but it does reduce overall cabinet space. Careful planning and an island help compensate for the lack of upper cabinets.

A.

B.

C

A) Stocked with the basic ingredients and tools needed for preparing meals, these two deep, sliding shelves function as a cook center in this kitchen. Storing items that you use together helps you work efficiently.

B) Although it isn't especially ornate or showy, this kitchen offers a full range of storage options: open shelves, dust-free storage behind glass doors, and numerous drawers and cupboards outfitted to meet specific storage needs.

C) Designed for efficient meal preparation, this cooking area includes generous work surfaces on both sides of the range as well as convenient storage for cooking oils above and spices below. The deep drawers on both sides of the range easily accommodate pots and pans along with other cooking supplies.

Remodeling Versus Adapting What You Have

Many people who seek better kitchen storage solutions start out wondering whether it makes more sense to remodel or to make better use of what already exists. There's no set answer, but one thing is clear: You can spend a lot of money on remodeling a kitchen yet wind up with storage systems that don't function any better than what you have now. Before you embark on a full-scale remodel, which may cost $50,000 or more, evaluate whether more modest changes might suffice. For $1,000 to $3,000, you can probably outfit your existing cabinets with a full line of storage accessories. Sometimes that's enough. In other houses, it would be a waste because underlying problems would remain.

A freestanding piece of furniture and simple bracket shelves provide additional kitchen storage without a major remodel.

Appearance. If the appearance of your cabinets is what bugs you, consider changing the look with paint or veneers of wood or laminate. You can also replace doors and drawer fronts, install new hardware, add or remove doors, or apply molding. The following pages will give you many ideas.

Floor plan. If the layout of your kitchen is problematic, you might need new cabinets. But first consider whether you might be able to simply add one cabinet, change the way doors swing, add shelves, or maybe get a cart that you can wheel in to provide more countertop space on busy baking days. Also remember that it's possible to move cabinets. You'll probably need new flooring and maybe new countertops, but you'll save money overall and create less waste than you would with a full renovation.

Wear. If doors won't close because numerous hinges have pulled out of the cabinet boxes or if drawers are falling apart, you probably do need to replace the cabinets, especially if the failed parts are made of particleboard. You might be able to repair solid wood. If only a few hinges are loose, glue wooden toothpicks in the stripped screw holes, wait for the glue to dry, drill new holes, and reinstall the hinges. If a door breaks, call the cabinet manufacturer (if you know who it is) to see whether a replacement is still available. Or check at a store that sells used building materials.

Budget. If you buy new cabinets, figure on spending $300 or more per door opening, including installation but not a countertop. Covering the existing surface with a veneer of thin wood or laminate starts at just half that, though costs escalate if the job is complex. Refinishing gets the cost down to about $50 per door opening if you pay a professional, or maybe $50 to $100 for the whole kitchen if you do it yourself.

A) **These new cabinets incorporate design elements** that you can use if you are updating existing cabinetry. The main lesson is that you don't have to make everything match. To avoid monotony, the designer chose cabinets of different heights, used glass doors on some, and left others open.

B) **Old and new not only coexist** comfortably in this kitchen but are the key to its success. The vintage cabinet converted into an island draws the most attention, but there are subtle touches too. Drawer fronts, for example, are different in the top drawers than they are in the lower drawers. This treatment is worth remembering if you decide to reconfigure existing cabinetry by converting shelf sections to drawers but can't find drawer fronts that match the ones you already own.

Recipes for an Efficient Kitchen

Over the years, people who design kitchens for a living have come up with some rules of thumb that help ensure efficient workspaces. The National Kitchen and Bath Association has distilled them into 40 guidelines, which you can read at www.nkba.org. Based on these guidelines, here are some things to think about as you evaluate what needs to be fixed in your current kitchen or incorporated into your plan for a new kitchen.

If your kitchen lacks counter space, consider adding a pullout cutting board (right).

When you're kneading bread or coaching a young cook on how to make brownies, it's helpful to have a counter a few inches lower than the usual 36 inches. This low island extension also provides storage space (below).

Cooking. Provide countertops on both sides of the range so that you have a place to set hot pots. Make one at least 15 inches wide and the other at least 12 inches wide. On an island or peninsula, allow at least 9 inches of counter behind a cooktop. You also need a counter at least 15 inches wide next to a wall oven or within 48 inches of it.

Refrigerator. The refrigerator door should open away from the main work area, and the door should have enough swing space so you can remove bins and shelves for cleaning. Provide a counter at least 15 inches wide next to the refrigerator. Put it on the handle side of a standard refrigerator or on either side of a side-by-side model.

Sink. The ideal spot for a sink is between the refrigerator and the range. Provide at least 24 inches of counter space on one side and 18 inches on the other. Place a garbage can nearby. The dishwasher should be within 36 inches of the sink. It's also helpful to have cabinets for clean dishes close by.

Clearances. Particularly in a busy kitchen there must be enough space between cabinets so people don't bump into each other. Standard minimum clearances are shown in the illustration above. The main meal preparation area needs at least 36 inches of countertop. If two cooks will be working together, they each need that much space.

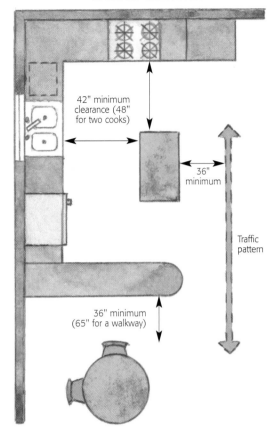

STANDARD CLEARANCES

42" minimum clearance (48" for two cooks)

36" minimum

Traffic pattern

36" minimum (65" for a walkway)

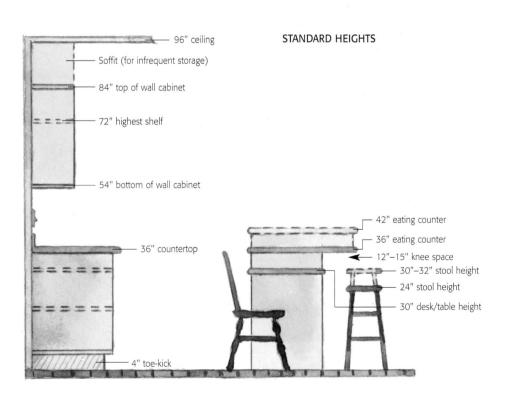

STANDARD HEIGHTS

96" ceiling
Soffit (for infrequent storage)
84" top of wall cabinet
72" highest shelf
54" bottom of wall cabinet
36" countertop
4" toe-kick

42" eating counter
36" eating counter
12"–15" knee space
30"–32" stool height
24" stool height
30" desk/table height

Deciding Between Open and Closed Storage

In some kitchens, everything stows away behind solid doors. In other kitchens, some or all of the storage space is in view on open shelves or behind glass doors. There are good reasons for each strategy. Fully enclosed storage makes life easy. You don't have to worry about tidiness, and the doors keep out dust. But open storage creates an airy, less formal look that better suits the style that many people want in a kitchen, and it lets visitors share in kitchen chores more easily. Half-and-half kitchens strike a good middle ground. In these, some cupboards have doors, while other spaces are open or perhaps covered with something that's a little cloudier than standard glass.

Etched glass or acrylic panels blur details but preserve the airy look that many people want when they select glass doors for cabinets.

Creating Blackboard Doors

Cabinet doors do more than hide things if you turn them into blackboards.

The switch is easy if existing doors are plywood or have a high-pressure laminate coating. Scuff up the surface with sandpaper and coat it with a primer labeled for use over slick surfaces. Top that with several coats of blackboard paint.

For frame-and-panel doors, make blackboards from hardboard cut to match the size of the existing panels. Attach the new panels with adhesive-backed hook-and-loop fasteners.

Standard blackboard paint holds up well as long as you apply multiple coats and wait the time listed on the label before you draw on it. Also consider magnetic chalkboard paint (see Resources, pages 188–189). Flexible magnets and rare-earth magnets (the neodymium type) hold well to it. Standard refrigerator magnets are too heavy.

A pantry door, and the walls to either side, can be turned into a blackboard.

A.

B.

C.

D.

A) Glass doors on two sides work especially well on a cabinet that separates a kitchen from a dining area. Besides allowing light to pass through, this arrangement lets you load the glassware from the kitchen side and retrieve it from the table side, saving unnecessary steps.

B) For a serene, tidy look, carefully choose what you store behind glass doors or on open shelves.

C) Without doors on the cabinets, this kitchen gains a relaxed, unpretentious look that encourages guests to join in preparing meals.

D) High shelves or soffit space above upper cabinets is a good place to store dishes, vases, or other pieces that you need only occasionally. However, the very fact that you seldom use them means they are likely to become covered with dust. Adding glass doors cuts down on your cleaning chores.

Designing Efficient Islands

Islands are a fixture of modern kitchens, but they play very different roles depending on how they are equipped. At their simplest, they are work surfaces or staging areas with storage underneath. Add a small sink and access to a compost bin, though, and an island evolves into a food preparation area. With a cooktop, an island becomes a cooking center. With an overhang so people can pull up chairs or stools, it becomes a breakfast bar or the prime spot for sampling hors d'oeuvres during a party.

Because an island is freestanding, save steps by building in storage space for whatever you will use there.

A.

Prep island. A prep island needs a sink, hand towel, compost bin, cutting board, knives, and appliances such as a blender and a food processor. You'll probably want to store heavy equipment on a movable shelf outfitted with an appliance lift so you won't have to lift the machine directly. Provide an electrical receptacle and store appliances nearby.

Cooking island. A cooking island should be designed around the cooktop and its venting needs. If you opt for an overhead hood, it rules out an overhead pot rack. But the other option, a downdraft fan, requires ducts that extend through the island, significantly reducing storage space. Besides storage for pots and pans, provide places to keep cooking oils and spices, hot pads, and utensils. If you have room, add storage for a few platters or large serving bowls.

B.

Breakfast bar. If used as a gathering spot for parties, an island doesn't need much in the way of storage. People will gather even if you shoo them away. But if you want the island to work as a breakfast bar or a lunch counter, store napkins, salt and pepper, and other essentials there. Provide an overhang so people in a chair or on a stool can tuck in their knees. If the island's countertop is the standard 36 inches high, people will be most comfortable on low stools. Standard chairs work best for surfaces 28 to 30 inches high. For counters 42 to 48 inches high, use bar stools.

C.

D.

E.

F.

A) Rolling carts make good islands, especially where space is tight or where storage needs change with the seasons. This petite version folds flat.

B) Tables make good islands, but they're much more useful when they incorporate storage space, such as the shallow drawer and shelf of this butcher-block island.

C) The ends of islands provide easily accessible storage space. In this kitchen, a microwave oven fits into one end of an island that's devoted mostly to meal preparation.

D) If you are designing an island that's both a prep space and dining center, consider elevating the serving area by 6 to 12 inches so diners are less likely to be sprayed with water. On this island, the elevated portion serves as a place for people to lean against as they offer tips to the cook.

E) You can store more than pots and pans and other kitchen supplies in an island. This one corrals food and water bowls for the family dog. Because they are set into cutouts in the bottom shelf, the bowls stay out of the way and don't tip over.

F) At any island, people who pull up a chair appreciate an overhang; it gives them a place to put their legs. A curved extension is more flexible because one more person can usually manage to crowd in. The curved shape also makes the kitchen seem more spacious.

Corner Solutions

Cabinets that meet at an inside corner create a vexing situation: What can be done with the space trapped at the back? The most elegant solution involves opening up one of the walls at the back and using the space for a cabinet in an adjoining room. But that involves custom modifications, so it's rarely done. Instead, most people either fill the back with rarely used items (perhaps guaranteeing that they'll never be used) or invest in accessories such as lazy Susans or racks that pivot and slide. Some complex systems do make access easier, but convenience comes at a price—often hundreds of dollars and in some cases nearly $1,000 just for the hardware. Some designs also significantly reduce your actual useable storage space.

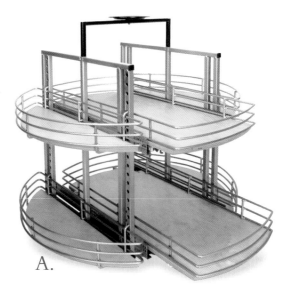

A.

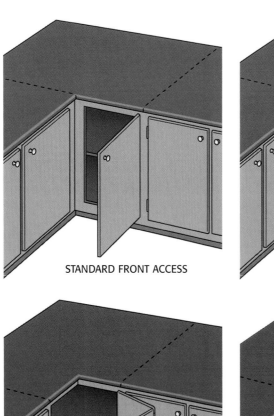

STANDARD FRONT ACCESS

DEAD-END CABINETS

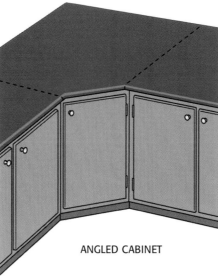

CORNER CABINET

ANGLED CABINET

Standard front-access shelves fill all the available space. Reaching into the back isn't easy, so consider storing seldom used items there in boxes or baskets. Pulling out a few containers is easier than rummaging at the back for the thing you want.

Dead-end cabinets end where they meet, even though the counter extends to the back corner. You lose use of the corner space, but what's left is all easy to reach.

A corner cabinet bridges the two straight runs of cabinets. A hinged door allows access. You can install simple shelves or a pie-shaped lazy Susan.

An angled cabinet is similar to a standard corner cabinet, but it extends across the corner at an angle, eliminating the need for a hinged door. You can install shelves, drawers, or a full-circle lazy Susan.

B.

C.

D.

E.

F.

A) A lazy Susan with pullout shelves revolves like a standard lazy Susan, but has center sections that pull out like sliding shelves.

B) A pie-shaped lazy Susan is the best option for a corner cabinet. Look for a high weight limit and tall sides so things don't tumble off the back.

C) These squiggle-shaped shelves pull out from standard front access cabinets and pivot in one smooth motion, bringing everything in the corner completely out of the cabinet.

D) Multiple-shelf units, which vary by manufacturer, are engineering marvels for standard front-access cabinets. Here, when you open the door, the shelves directly behind it pull out automatically. The back section, normally housed in the corner, moves into view. You can also pull out those shelves to gain easy access to what's in the back.

E) This half-moon lazy Susan is another option for standard front-access cabinets. The curved shape moves out automatically when the door opens and brings items from the back into view.

F) Angled drawers look like standard drawers when they are pushed in. You get about as much storage space as there is on a lazy Susan, and it's easier to reach.

Bringing Order Under the Sink

The space under the kitchen sink is a challenge. So many plumbing parts are in the way that it often becomes a dark cave. Yet it's a shame not to exploit the full storage potential of this prime location, where door racks, sliding shelves, and other organizing accessories work wonders.

Tilting drawers, door racks, stacking shelves, and plastic buckets filled with cleaning supplies bring order to this cabinet.

A) Numerous styles of sliding shelves work well under sinks. This version features a top shelf higher than most, so you can use it as a handle without stooping. The bottom sections are designed to hold bottles and jugs. The trays lift out for cleaning, and a tall wire cage keeps them from tipping.

B) This sliding shelf is better for short, wide items.

C) A U-shaped sliding shelf fits around pipes, water filters, and other plumbing parts. You can screw it to the cabinet sides at whatever height you want, though it won't work on sink cabinets that have a center post.

Hand Towel Options

Avoid dripping water throughout the kitchen by keeping a hand towel within reach.

A.

B.

C.

A) **Install a pullout rack** or even a simple bar so you can store hand towels behind closed doors.

B) **Mount a towel bar or a cup hook** to base cabinets or an island.

C) **If you use paper towels,** you can store them on a rack attached to the bottom of upper cabinets.

Sponge Savers

One challenge in any busy kitchen is where to store sponges, scrub pads, and other cleaning aids. Because they're often damp, you can't just toss them into a standard drawer with other kitchen tools. The best solution depends on whether you want to keep them within sight or hidden away.

D.

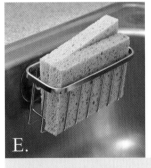

E.

F.

D) **Even the shallow space** between the front of the cabinet and the sink can be put to use. This panel tips forward to open. Look for easy-to-clean, removable liners.

E) **Storing sponges in the open air** helps them dry faster. This basket has suction cups that hold it to the sink.

F) **Instead of tilting forward,** this sponge drawer pulls out, along with a slightly deeper drawer to the side.

Storing Dishes and Glassware

Some people want to keep their dishes and glassware on display, while others prefer to tuck everything away. Whichever approach best suits your style, you'll want to protect dishes from chips. Simple approaches that don't require extra effort work best. Since the edges of plates and the rims of glasses are where most chips occur, it makes sense to focus on protecting them. Some people slip felt pads between stacked plates, but this usually isn't necessary, as the flat part of the plate isn't what chips. The solutions shown here are simple and effective.

A.

Build Your Own Plate Rack

Two ladder-like pieces with ⅜-inch dowels as rungs are all you need to make a plate rack custom-sized to your dishes and cabinets.

1 Cut four pieces of clear (knot-free) wood about ¾ inch by 1½ inches to fit the width of the opening.

2 Determine how many dowels you need, based on your cabinet's width and how many plates you want to store. Space dowel centers about 1½ to 2 inches apart across the shelf width.

3 Measure the vertical distance between shelves and subtract ¾ inch. Cut the dowels to this length.

4 Drill holes ⅜ inch in diameter and ⅜ inch deep in the cross-pieces for each dowel. Glue the dowels into the holes.

5 Using your plates as a guide for the spacing, screw one ladder into the cabinet near the back and the other near the front.

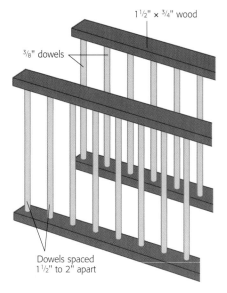

1½" × ¾" wood

⅜" dowels

Dowels spaced 1½" to 2" apart

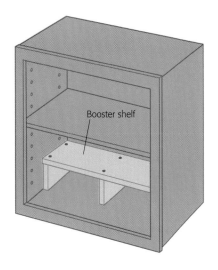

Booster shelf

Homemade Booster Shelves

With one board and a few screws, you can make a custom booster shelf that efficiently stores short glasses and cups.

1 Cut a board so one side fits loosely across the inside of the cabinet. Also cut two or three short pieces to serve as legs.

2 Drill pilot holes through the shelf into the legs.

3 Screw the shelf to the legs and slide the unit into place. For a face-frame cabinet or one with a center post, you may need to assemble the piece inside the cabinet.

A) When shelves are too far apart, you're likely to either waste space or stack dishware too high. Booster shelves are a better solution. There are many styles, including ones made of metal, thick wire, or plastic. You can also make your own—see the bottom illustration on page 102.

B) Suspended from their bases, wine and cocktail glasses hang safely in a cabinet. You can also install a rack like this beneath an upper cabinet.

C) Practical as well as decorative, a plate rack puts pottery on view while keeping pieces easily accessible and chip-free. The rack also allows you to put dishes away even if they are damp, as they can easily air-dry. Some racks are independent wall-hung units, while others fit between shelves in open cabinets.

D) If you reserve the walls of your kitchen for windows or artwork, you may decide to store dishes in drawers. Sturdy wooden pegs, secured into holes in a base piece, keep dishes from knocking against each other every time you open or close the drawer.

E) Deciding how to store dishes and glassware isn't an either/or proposition. You can combine several approaches and use them as part of your decorating scheme. In this kitchen, simple shelves hold plates and bowls, while cups hang from hooks on a rail. Glasses and other dishes are kept behind glass doors.

Storing Silverware

With silverware, you may have dozens of pieces but just a handful of types. Using the right storage system makes it easy to sort pieces as you put them away. Not all ready-made drawer organizers have the same number of compartments, so choose partly by what you have in your silverware collection. For most people, the minimum includes two compartments for spoons (small and soup-size), two for forks (salad and main-course) and one for knives. Additional compartments let you store serving spoons and assorted specialty pieces, such as long-handle spoons that you use with iced tea, or spoons with a knife edge for cutting out sections of grapefruit.

How to Make Your Own Drawer Dividers

In less time than you might spend shopping for the right size drawer divider, you can make one that fits your needs exactly. This version has no bottom, so it's easy to clean. If you prefer a closed base, use 1/4-inch plywood or melamine-coated hardboard.

1 Design a layout that includes T intersections but not X's.

2 Cut sides to match the drawer's length, minus 1/8 inch or so, and front and back pieces to match the drawer's width, minus 7/8 inch, assuming you are using wood 3/8 inch thick. (Cutting slightly undersize gives you a little wiggle room.) Also cut interior pieces. Shorten those that butt into others by 3/4 inch to allow for the overlap at both ends.

3 Drill pilot holes for two screws at each joint, then assemble the divider. You don't need glue.

Helpful Hint

If you outfit a silverware drawer with a series of shallow boxes rather than a tray with compartments, tack the containers to each other with adhesive-backed hook-and-loop fasteners so they don't shift position.

3/8" by 2"

Front

Screws

Protecting Silver from Tarnish

If you own utensils that are silver or silver plated and don't use them often, consider storing them in a case made of tarnish-inhibiting cloth. Or simply wrap the pieces in this material, which you can find at some fabric shops. It absorbs airborne sulfur compounds so they don't cause a black layer to form on your silverware. Humidity also contributes to tarnishing, so keep the case in a clear plastic bag made of Mylar or polyethylene. Museum conservators suggest using bags made for roasting turkeys. Never store silver in PVC bags, as the plastic releases chemicals. Tarnish does not damage silver directly, but it's still important to prevent it because polishing silver to remove tarnish wears away part of the surface.

A.

B.

C.

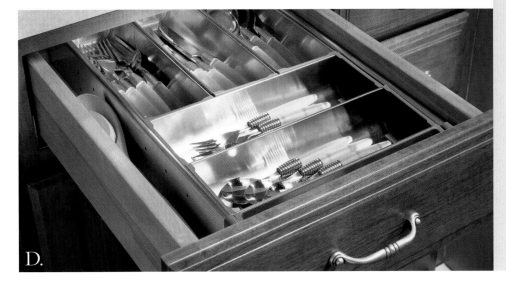

D.

A) To make setting the table a breeze, consider storing at least a meal's worth of silverware and napkins in a tote. This approach makes even more sense when you're dining in another room or heading out to enjoy a meal on a patio.

B) If you have drawers that are custom sizes, look for adjustable silverware organizers. The type shown here has parts that slide together. You can also find drawer dividers made of plastic and cut them to size with scissors.

C) Piggybacking two drawers in the space of one allows you to keep different sets of silverware separate. Or you can store silverware in one section and meal-preparation tools in the other. In the double drawer shown here, the top section slides on runners mounted inside the bottom drawer.

D) If your silverware has oversized handles or if you have numerous pieces, look for drawer organizers with deep bins, or outfit the drawer with bread pans or other suitable containers.

Storing Cooking Utensils

Your cooking utensil collection may be just as large as your assortment of silverware, but the individual components come in many sizes and shapes. So for cooking utensils, it is usually practical to have a more flexible storage system that loosely groups them by type.

Storing Knives

Knife storage must be safe, and it should help keep blades from dulling. If young children are in your house, store sharp tools above their reach. A knife block at the back of the counter is probably safe when children are very young, but as they grow, you might need to find a higher spot.

How to Make a Knife Block

1 From a 4-foot-long piece of 2-by-8-inch wood, cut grooves down the length. Make the grooves slightly wider than the knife blades, and space them a bit farther apart than the thickness of the handles.

2 Cut the board into equal lengths.

3 Glue and clamp them together with the grooves aligned.

To store wooden spoons and other cooking tools, one of the easiest solutions also works best: Stash them in a wide canister that you leave next to the stove.

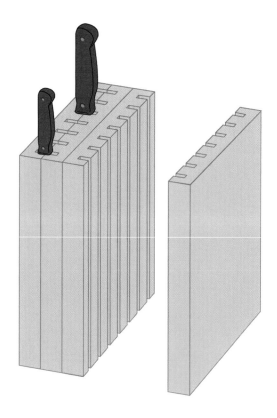

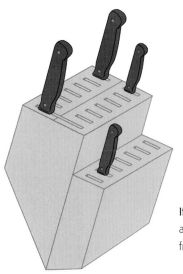

If you want the block tilted so knives are easier to remove, adapt these directions so you wind up with a small block in front that stabilizes the main knife block in back.

A.

B.

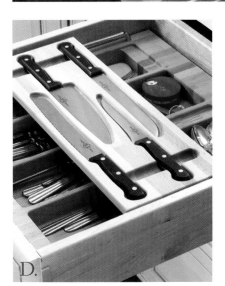

C.

D.

E.

A) This type of rack pulls down from the base of an upper cabinet, a location that keeps knives where they are handy for a cook but beyond the reach of young children.

B) A narrow pullout knife rack can fit between cabinets. This space is often covered over with a filler strip rather than used for storage.

C) In kitchens where toddlers don't go, knives can be stored in drawers. The wooden knife block at the back of this drawer has a dozen thin slits, each designed to cradle a knife blade and prevent it from rattling against others. Combining knife storage and a cutting surface is clever, provided you remember to extend the board over stored knives when you chop. Otherwise, bits of food will likely tumble down into the drawer.

D) You can also store knives sideways in a sliding tray at the top of a utensil drawer.

E) Because cooking utensils have varied shapes, larger compartments allow you to store more items in a drawer than you could if it were divided into smaller sections. The pieces settle in next to each other so that the outward bulge on one item fills an inward curve on the next.

Storing Pots, Pans, and Trays

Pots and pans are bulky and often difficult to stack, and their handles tend to poke out in different directions. There's also the challenge of organizing the lids for quick access to the one you need. Trays are thin but large. There are many ways to store these items. The key is to be efficient by keeping pots and pans under the cooktop or next to the range. Trays tend to be used less frequently, so they can be farther away.

How to Make a Lid Tray

Use this insert in a drawer.

1 From a 1-by-6-inch pine board, cut slats long enough to span the depth of the drawer minus 1½ inches.

2 Cut two end pieces to the width of the drawer.

3 With a pencil, lightly mark end pieces with a centerline for each slat. Angle the lines about 40 degrees up from the base. Adjust the angle, if necessary, so lids fit within the drawer depth.

4 About 1 inch from the top and bottom of each end piece, drill two pilot holes through each line. Screw through the holes to attach the end pieces to the slats.

A.

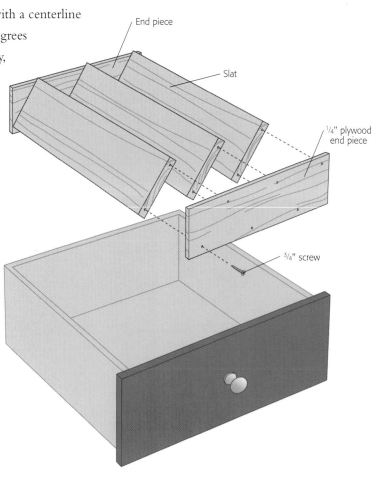

End piece

Slat

¼" plywood end piece

¾" screw

Helpful Hint

Besides trays and pans, vertical dividers can store cutting boards. Get a divider with enough openings to separate the cutting surfaces. This speeds drying, an important sanitary step that causes any bacteria on the board to die off or at least not multiply.

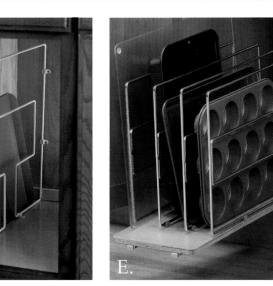

A) This slide-out organizer, with its own slide-out shelf and side compartments, fits in a standard base cabinet and holds a whole set of cookware. You can even stow cookie sheets on one side.

B) Drawer dividers help bring order to deep compartments. Besides allowing you to stow different types of pots or other gear in specific areas, dividers keep lids upright so you can easily pick out the one you need.

C) Similar to a rack you'd use to air-dry dishes, this pullout shelf for wide base cabinets contains numerous slots that allow upright storage of thin cookware, including frying pans, lids, and cookie sheets.

D) A vertical divider in a cabinet lets you store cookie sheets and large trays on their sides. This saves space and allows you to remove a tray without having to maneuver it out of a stack.

E) Pullout vertical dividers are even easier to use.

Pot Racks

Instead of stowing pots in cupboards and drawers, you can display them in your kitchen. This makes it easy to find the size you want, and it frees up considerable space for other things. Plus, it makes a kitchen look like a chef's workshop. Many restaurant chefs hang their pots, and it was the solution favored by world-renowned chef Julia Child. Faced with an enormous collection of cookware, she hung sauté pans and other relatively shallow types on hooks or on a pegboard on walls. She hoisted pots onto a rack over her range.

Before you invest in a pot rack, though, also consider the downsides. If some cooks in your kitchen are much taller than others, the rack is likely to hang out of one person's reach or block someone else's view. You'll still need to store lids and deep pots, and you might find yourself spending more time scrubbing the bottoms of pots than you do now.

How big should a pot rack be? Especially when a pot rack hangs over an island, it's important to get the right size. One that's too big puts pots where they can bump your head and block your view. One that's too small or too high puts them beyond easy reach.

■ **Height.** Stand a few feet out from a wall and mark where you touch it when you are reaching forward at a comfortable height, as if you were grabbing a pot from a rack. Measure up from that point to the ceiling. This is the total distance you have for the hanging mechanism, the rack, and the dangling pans. Small pots usually need 10 inches, while a 10-inch skillet with a handle may need 21 inches. You might have to settle on an average.

■ **Length and width.** For aesthetic reasons as well as further insurance against bumping your head, get a pot rack that's at least 6 inches smaller all around than the island it will hang over.

A.

B.

A) If you hang a pot rack over an island cooktop, consider one with built-in lights. Besides preventing clutter on the ceiling, this helps ensure that the rack doesn't block much of the light.

B) You can also mount a rack on a wall. Look for a model that allows you to hang pots a ways out so they don't scuff up the wall. Because of the cantilever, these racks also need to transfer weight to the wall. The top straps perform that function on the rack shown here, but bracing could angle down underneath instead.

C) In a kitchen where an island has overhead ventilation, a pot rack can be set up in an alcove in a section of cabinets.

D) Customize a pot rack by surrounding it with molding that matches the cabinets in your kitchen.

E) Pot racks help create an open look in a kitchen and signal that everyone is welcome to share in preparing a meal.

Storing Small Appliances

So-called small appliances don't always seem so small when you're trying to find a place to store them. Blenders and food processors are too tall to fit between some shelves, and stand mixers are heavy as well. Plus there are all the special attachments these appliances require.

Instead of packing all of this gear into one prime kitchen storage space, consider keeping various appliances on shelves or in deep drawers along with other supplies that you tend to use at the same time. For example, if you use your blender mostly to prepare drinks when you entertain, you might want to store it with wine and glasses in a cabinet that doubles as a bar. A mixer or food processor could go next to the countertop where you prepare food.

If you don't like lifting heavy appliances and setting them down, install hardware that does the work for you. Or store the appliances at counter height in an appliance garage and scoot them out as needed.

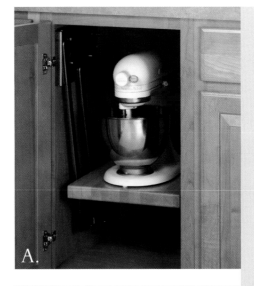

A.

B.

A) Equipped with a heavy-duty lift mechanism, this shelf and a mixer stow away in a standard base cabinet.

B) When it's time to bake a cake, press a couple of levers and pull up. The shelf and mixer pivot out and rise to nearly the height of the countertop. Though mixers weigh 20 to 25 pounds, very little strength is needed to operate the lift. You can use the mixer without taking it off the shelf, provided an electrical receptacle is near.

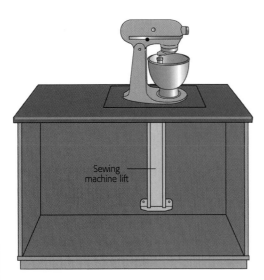

Sewing machine lift

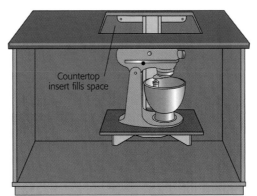

Countertop insert fills space

By using a sewing machine lift instead of an appliance lift, you can have the mixer rise up within the countertop. These lifts (see Resources, pages 188–189) typically support 40 pounds and include a gas-filled cylinder and a cable that do the work. You'll need to cut a trap door in the countertop, however, so this idea is more feasible with some countertop materials than with others.

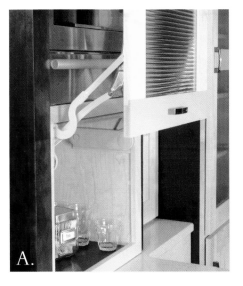

A.

B.

C.

D.

Door options for appliance garages.

An appliance garage lets you hide a mixer, toaster, or other piece of equipment behind a door at the back of a counter. The way the door opens makes a difference in how you can use the surrounding space.

A) **Lift-up doors** let you reach the appliance and leave things on the counter, but they block access to shelves or cabinets above.

B) **Tambour doors,** which roll up out of sight like the cover on a rolltop desk, give you the option of switching between open and closed cabinets whenever you want.

C) **Bifold doors fold in half,** reducing swing space but not eliminating it.

D) **A flipper door pivots up and in,** similar to the way doors on TV cabinets often work. The countertop remains free, and the door doesn't block storage above.

Storing Spices

Storing spices is easy if you limit your cooking to one cuisine. But if you venture out and explore all the flavors of the world, your storage needs grow dramatically.

Arrangement. If you have a big collection of spices, keeping them in alphabetical order helps you find what you want quickly. If you have too many spices for one rack, set them out alphabetically and figure out which groupings make the most sense. Because many spices happen to start with the letter C, you might find that it works best to put all the C's together and have separate racks for the rest.

Freshness. Whatever solution you ultimately select, it's important to recognize that spices retain their flavor best when you keep them away from heat, moisture, and direct sunlight. There's no safety issue involved—you won't get sick from eating stale spices—so you can make trade-offs that best suit your needs. For example, you might store spices next to the range, where they are easy to reach when you're cooking, even though they will grow stale sooner because of the heat. If flavor is paramount, you might purchase spices as whole seeds whenever possible and grind them to order. Whole seeds retain flavor longer than ground spices do. Mark the month and year on spices when you buy them. As they age, keep their effect on recipes constant by gradually increasing the amount you use.

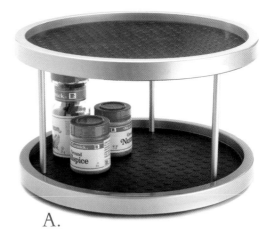

A.

B.

How Long Do Spices Stay Fresh?

Spice seller McCormick & Company suggests these guidelines, assuming good storage conditions. For best color and flavor, store red-pepper products, including paprika and chili powder, in a refrigerator.

Ground spices	2–3 years
Whole spices	3–4 years
Herbs	1–3 years
Seeds	3–4 years
Seasoning blends	1–2 years
Extracts	4 years

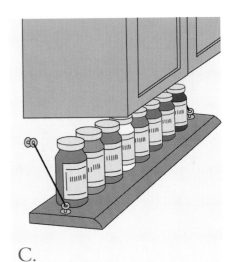

C.

D.

E.

F.

G.

H.

A) **A double turntable,** similar to a lazy Susan, keeps spices on two levels. You can twirl the unit to bring containers at the back within reach. Some turntables allow you to adjust the height of the top shelf.

B) **There are many designs** for free-standing spice racks that can be left on a countertop. This version spins.

C) **With a couple of eye hooks,** a little twine or chain, and a board, you can make a spice shelf that hangs below upper cabinets.

D) **Angled inserts let you see labels** but limit how many containers fit in a drawer.

E) **Store three times as many jars** in a drawer by placing them upright. Label the lids for easy identification. If standard spice jars are too tall for your drawer, buy shorter ones or substitute baby food jars. New parents usually have plenty of those to give away.

F) **Stair-step shelves** hold spices in rows of different heights so you can see the labels. You sacrifice a little storage space because the shelves need to be farther apart than they might otherwise be.

G) **A door-mounted rack** makes spices easy to see and reach. Usually you'll find room for a rack like this without adjusting the shelves in the cabinet. In some cases you might need to trim off a small amount from the back of each shelf.

H) **This pullout rack** is built in to one of the pillars that flank a cooktop and support its ventilation hood. The cook can reach spices easily, yet most of the time they're sheltered from heat, light, and food spatters. Both sides of each shelf are accessible.

Storing Wine

The more wine you have, the more careful you need to be about storage conditions, because it's likely to be a while before you open all those bottles. A few requirements are easy to meet, even if you don't have a dedicated wine storage area. Place bottles on their sides or upside down so the corks don't dry out. Choose an area that isn't likely to vibrate when a washer spins or kids tromp up and down stairs. And stay away from heating vents and bright light, especially direct sunlight. Ideally, the storage temperature should be around 55 degrees, but even 70 is acceptable, especially if it doesn't fluctuate much. Relative humidity should be around 50 percent.

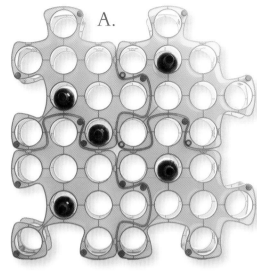

A.

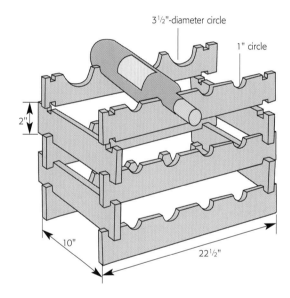

3½"-diameter circle

1" circle

Scallop racks, with half-round notches in pairs of boards, are a popular way to store wine. These supports, which you can buy or make, fit in freestanding racks or in shelves or drawers.

2"

10"

22½"

B.

C.

D.

E.

F.

G.

H.

A) A fun take on what has become a very serious pursuit for some people, this puzzle-shaped wine rack comes in sections that hook together.

B) Boards that interlock to form an X are the basis of this design, one of the most popular ways to store wine. You can use a single X, as shown here, or combine several in a larger cabinet.

C) Some X-shaped wine racks are made of thin lattice pieces at the front and back of a cabinet. With these, you store one bottle in each section. The bottles are easy to retrieve, but the lattice is relatively fragile.

D) For people who have the space, a wine cellar is the ultimate indulgence. This setup provides square-shaped cubbies for narrow bottles and X-shaped holders for wider bottles.

E) Slanting shelves as well as a pull-out drawer equip a narrow space so it can store more than two dozen bottles.

F) A wine rack can be attached to the bottom of a cabinet or shelf, saving space on the counter or in the cabinet.

G) Simple pigeonholes also work for storing wine. The shape also adapts to other uses, such as filing outgoing mail. Compartments like this are easy to work into a section of cabinets or to incorporate into an island.

H) Call it a tasting table, or add a bigger overhang and call it an island. Either way, the lattice-style base holds 216 bottles on their sides.

Pantries

In many ways, walk-in pantries could be considered the perfect storage space. Most pantry shelves are inexpensive, especially compared with kitchen cabinets, so you get a lot of storage space for your money. It's easily accessible too, especially if you include a stepstool so you can reach high shelves. Another charm of a pantry is its utilitarian nature. You can stack things on the floor, hang totes from hooks, or make other modifications to suit your changing needs.

Built as swinging storage, the end doors in this run of cabinets hold a fair amount of food on shelves and in a small drawer. But when you open the doors, you realize that's just the beginning. Behind them is a full walk-in pantry. The top half of each door is open on both sides so air circulates and items are accessible from either side.

A.

B.

C.

D.

A) **Wide and narrow shelves,** some closely spaced and some quite far apart, provide a variety of storage options in this pantry. The open shelves make good use of the corner space, which would be difficult to reach into if the shelves were covered by doors.

B) **Modular storage,** such as this bracket-and-standard system, works well in walk-in pantries. Look for a setup that accommodates additional shelves, drawers, stacking shelves, or other features so you can customize the pantry to meet your changing needs.

C) **Swinging doors allow air** to circulate—a necessity in pantries that store potatoes, onions, or other produce. Saloon-style doors solve the problem of how to get in and out when your arms are loaded with food or other supplies.

D) **Glass-fronted drawers** for grains and pasta, high cubbies for platters, and open shelving keep supplies well organized in this walk-in pantry.

Cabinet Pantries

If there's no place for a walk-in pantry, you can achieve some of the same benefits by outfitting cabinets so they're more accessible.

A.

B.

C.

Narrow shelves cover the two main doors as well as the two interior doors of this deep pantry cabinet. The setup puts almost every item in the front at least part of the time.

A) Sliding shelves are the simplest upgrade. They're particularly useful on deep shelves, where things in the back otherwise tend to be forgotten. Sliding shelves often have relatively low sides, so use baskets or boxes to keep small items together or to prevent bottles from tipping.

B) A pullout pantry takes the sliding-shelf idea one step further. Instead of opening a door and then pulling out individual shelves, you slide all or most of the storage system out in one step.

C) Tandem shelves, designed to fit in a tall, narrow cabinet, essentially split a deep space in half, giving even the back of the cabinet front-row status.

D.

E.

F.

D) A swivel-type pantry can be turned once it's pulled out from a cabinet. This feature is especially useful next to a wall, where there wouldn't be room to stand to retrieve items from one side.

E) A floor-to-ceiling pantry closet turns a hard-to-use corner into efficient storage space. The wavy glass doors obscure the labels but still let light through—a great solution when the pantry area has a window that you don't want to block off from the kitchen.

F) A base-cabinet pantry includes door racks, sliding shelves, and pullout shelves, all bringing storage within easy reach.

Garbage and Recycling

In most kitchens, the garbage can is under the sink. But before you settle on that spot, take a quick look around the room. If most food preparation occurs somewhere else—at an island counter, for example—it might make more sense to get rid of the waste there. A single garbage can probably won't do either, because there are many more opportunities to recycle waste than there once were. If your community recycles only items that have been sorted by type, you'll want to provide enough containers so that people can sort as they toss.

A.

B.

With pullout bins, you can set up a recycling center right in the kitchen—a convenience that helps family members actually remember to use it.

C.

A) **Stacking bins allow you** to convert a base cabinet or a tall cabinet into a recycling center.

B) **A slide-out shelf carries a garbage can** along for the ride. This one has a clip that holds the container steady.

C) **Garbage cans can also slide on rails** attached to drawer slides. This holds the can steadier but puts the hardware closer to food scraps than it is with a slide-out shelf, so the mechanism is more likely to need periodic cleaning.

D) **A foot pedal allows you** to summon a slide-out garbage can even if your hands are full.

E) **A plastic-bag holder can help** if you use grocery bags as trash can liners. Attach the bag holder to the door nearest the one that hides the garbage can.

F) **This four-bin** recycling center runs on door slides and includes two closed containers. You might use one for vegetable scraps headed to a compost pile and the other for standard garbage. The big bins are perfect for cans, bottles, or paper.

G) **With this type of door-mounted garbage can,** opening the door makes the can swing out for easy access and automatically lifts its lid. When you close the door, the can scoots back in and the lid shuts.

dining rooms

t may be time to rethink how you use your dining room. If you use it only occasionally, you may be able to solve storage problems in other rooms by shifting something to the dining area. Done carefully, this will still leave you with a fully functional dining room for holiday dinners and other events. Possible features include a mail-sorting station, a pantry housed in an armoire, a small home office, or a computer center for the family. A dining room is also a great place to store serving platters and fine china.

Even when you use a dining room for meals, it can still play other roles. The architect who worked on this house refers to this as the breakfast room, but it stays in use throughout the day. Behind the closed doors, the cabinets provide abundant storage. There's also a functional home office with a TV hidden in the compartment above the computer, as well as a bar complete with a temperature- and humidity-controlled wine cooler. The cabinet on the far right is large enough to function as a pantry for a busy family. Even the table has built-in storage. Its shallow drawers are just the right size for placemats.

A) You can ease a dining room into a double life by designing new storage so that it resembles traditional dining room furniture. In this room, the arch over the counter and the glass doors on the cupboards make the cabinets resemble a hutch. The storage wall also incorporates a small home office.

B) Bookshelves and base cabinets create more of a library feeling in this Colonial-style dining room.

C) A home library is a good match for a dining room because books add warmth and intimacy. In this room, people are likely to be so drawn to the books that they might not notice the substantial amount of enclosed storage below. Because the lower area is not within view, it can house anything without impinging on the room's dining function. Consider using at least some of that space for table linens, candles, and serving pieces.

bedrooms

Some people see a bedroom as the ultimate personal oasis, a place to refresh and recharge for the next busy day. For other people, a bedroom is merely a place to sleep, dress, and store clothes. Whichever camp you're in, you may find it a struggle to keep order in a bedroom. It's just too easy to leave clothes lying about in a room that's generally not on display. But meeting a few basic storage requirements goes a long way toward preventing chaos.

Nightstand. At the head of the bed beside each person, provide enough space for a book or magazine, a glass of water, and an alarm clock. Though any flat surface will do as a nightstand, furniture or built-ins that incorporate more storage space can be helpful, especially where books or magazines tend to pile up. If space is tight in your house, consider using a chair with a wooden seat that you can use as a spare when guests arrive.

Reading light. Regardless of what other light sources exist in the room, put a light for each person at the right height to read in bed. The light can be placed on a nightstand or mounted to the wall above it. The bottom of the shade should be about 20 inches above the pillow. Any lower and there won't be enough light on pages; any higher and the bulb will shine in your eyes.

Clothes. Hanging space and drawers need to be adequate for the amount of clothing you store. What that means depends on the person and the storage system's efficiency. Most people use both a bureau and a closet, but if the closet includes drawers, it might be all you need. For more about closets, see pages 138–145.

Guest Bedrooms

Guest bedrooms have most of the same requirements as main ones, but they don't need as much storage space. Unless visitors stay for long periods, you can probably convert the closet to another use. It might be a good place to store old legal papers, holiday decorations, or crafts materials. Or you can outfit the closet with a desk and bookcase and use it as a home office. But plan ahead so you don't have to scramble to make space for guests.

A chest with extra bedding (left) allows guests to add or remove covers to suit their preferences.

A small auxiliary closet, like the one below, can be a useful addition to a guest bedroom if you convert the main closet to another purpose.

A.

B.

C.

A) **This built-in bookcase** provides a nice side benefit: a sturdy backrest for reading in bed.

B) **In a room** with an unusually high ceiling, a tall cabinet creates a more sheltered spot for the bed.

C) **When a bedroom closet** doesn't have room for shoe storage, consider an independent shoe rack. To make one similar to this, nail or screw one or two shelves between the legs of a simple bench. Add a vertical divider to help keep the shelves from sagging.

Adding Storage Under a Bed

If you want to add storage capacity to a bedroom, one obvious place is that big gap that's usually under the bed. The space might not be very high, but it's long and wide, dimensions that can be hard to find elsewhere. For storing holiday wrap, kids' artwork, toys, or spare linens and blankets, it could be perfect.

If the floor in your bedroom is carpeted, you can probably just slide boxes in and out. With other kinds of flooring, particularly if you store heavy items, consider getting drawers with glides or containers with wheels. Dust tends to collect in the still space under a bed, so select containers with covers.

Although it's relatively easy to build your own under-bed storage, you probably won't save much money unless you have spare materials already on hand. Many low-cost, ready-made options are available at stores that specialize in storage materials. Before you invest in an under-bed system, measure the height available and check for obstructions, such as a center bar on a wide bed.

Long rolls of wrapping paper and fluffy ribbon bouquets fit easily under a bed. Using clear plastic containers allows you to see what's in each box.

If you want to use wooden boxes under a bed, consider adding wheels and handholds, especially if the flooring is something other than carpet. Wheels make heavy boxes easier to move, and they help keep the floor from getting scratched.

Under-bed storage containers are available in a variety of styles. Some consist of archival-quality cardboard, making them ideal for storing keepsakes and textiles. This one is mostly fabric, although the zip-down lid is clear plastic.

Dealing with Dirty Laundry

Minimize laundry by providing a place to put clothes you've just worn, particularly if you plan to wear them again before washing them. Pegs or hooks work well, or try a spare chair. Anything is better than the floor, as a cluttered floor signals that people don't need to be neat because the room is already out of control. For clothes that need to be washed, provide a hamper or an open basket that allows air to circulate.

Choose a container that is easy to move to the laundry area. If many of your clothes need to be folded, look for a container that is also suitable for carting clean clothes back to the room.

A classic laundry basket transports dirty clothes to the wash and clean clothes back to bedrooms.

This folding hamper features a cotton bag that can go in the wash too when necessary.

Besides holding dirty or clean laundry, an attractive hamper can provide overflow storage, perhaps for bulky sweaters that are brought out only during winter.

Built-in Bedroom Storage

Adding bookshelves and cabinets to a bedroom can solve more than storage problems. You can also use built-ins to create a cozier room or to divide a large room into a sleeping area and one that you use for another purpose, such as a home office or a hobby room. Built-ins can go along a wall, or they can function as a wall. When they are room dividers, you can incorporate storage on both sides.

In this bedroom, a built-in cabinet serves as a headboard and a room divider, separating the space into sleeping and dressing areas. The ends of the cabinet include bookshelves, and the back is outfitted as a dresser.

Beyond Built-ins

If you can't afford built-in bedroom storage, or if it isn't practical, you still have many options in addition to closets and standard bureaus. To get more hanging space, for example, you can install a high bracket shelf with a rod or a series of Shaker pegs. As a room divider, an armoire works as well as a built-in. A low bench with cubbies can store books or shoes.

Wall-mounted shelves with pegs and side-by-side shoe cubbies add storage space in this bedroom.

A.

B.

C.

A) **The wall at the head** of a bed can become one giant storage space. The head of this bed tucks into a central niche. Besides providing a good place to attach reading lights, the recess makes the space seem more intimate. The bed itself sits on a platform containing drawers.

B) **Past the foot of the bed**, a freestanding cabinet divides the room into two spaces and extends the line of the fireplace. The side facing the bed functions as a bureau and television cabinet.

C) **The other side** of the storage unit incorporates bookshelves. Along with a desk, they create a home office.

Building Storage into a Bed

Where space is especially tight, it often makes sense to incorporate storage space into a bed. You may need to trade away a little convenience, because the bed may become slightly higher than usual and the storage may be so low that you need to crouch to use it. But in return, you'll gain spacious drawers or shelves.

Pullout Cart or Nightstand

If you're considering a built-in bed in a guest room, think about leaving space for a handy rollout cart. Tucked away, it will blend in with the bed and require no floor space. But when guests arrive, it pulls out and gives them a place to open a suitcase. You could also use this concept to create a tuck-away nightstand where you normally need clear space alongside a bed.

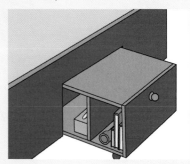

Instead of a footboard, a storage chest anchors this bed. But it's not for blankets or pillows. The plants come off and up pops the TV.

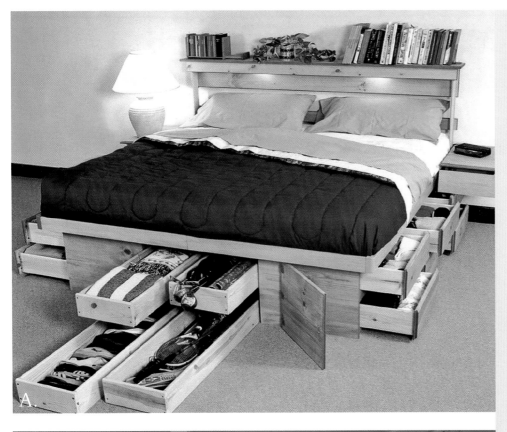

A) Besides having storage in its headboard and two side tables, this bed fits a whole dresser's worth of drawers under its mattress. This double-layer, king-size version sits 18 inches high and has 12 drawers, one of which is long enough for skis. A single-layer version is 9 inches high and has six drawers.

B) A built-in bed is often called a captain's bed. Think of this as a co-captain's setup. Besides sleeping space for two people, it has a double layer of storage options underneath. Recessing the lower drawers creates a toe-kick, making it easier for someone to reach across while changing the sheets. It also provides space for slippers.

Children's Rooms

In every room, clearing out clutter is the first step when you are trying to find better storage solutions. That's especially true in a child's room. The toy that's fascinating today is often ignored tomorrow. But before you get rid of anything, consider whether time away from certain toys might rekindle a child's interest in them. Many parents find that by rotating toys, they keep clutter to a reasonable level and have a way to bring out something "new" periodically without buying anything.

Low shelving is one of the best storage options in a child's room. Everything is visible and easily accessible, unlike with the classic deep toy box, where a child needs to pull out everything to get what's at the bottom. While shelves are always good for books, they also work well for individual toys, stuffed animals, and dolls.

Bins and boxes. Bins are the best storage option for collections of small things that are in frequent use, such as construction toys or doll clothes. Because the fronts are open, bins are as easy to use as shelves, yet they keep things in semi-enclosed containers. Children can still see what's inside, and they don't have to open doors or close lids.

Baskets and boxes without lids work well as catchalls for large items, such as balls or stuffed animals. Mesh baskets, which allow kids to see what's inside without emptying everything, are particularly useful.

Pegs and hooks. These simple storage devices are also easy for kids to use. Encourage them to hang up clothes that have been worn but don't yet need laundering. Kids can also use pegs for hats, jackets, backpacks, and even mesh bags filled with collections of toys.

When children are young and space in a house is tight, the closets in their rooms sometimes need to be devoted to other uses. In such cases, you can substitute space in a freestanding cabinet. Because children's clothing doesn't require much hanging space, this armoire is outfitted with high and low shelves. A row of clips on the door can hold mittens.

A.

B.

C.

A) Unless you want to buy new furniture or remodel every few years, choose main storage systems that are relatively age-neutral. In this room for two, each child gets a large bookcase with drawers below, plus one more drawer under the window seat. All of these are just as useful to a 6-year-old as they are to a 16-year-old.

B) With secondary storage units, you're freer to indulge in gear that will eventually be outgrown. In this toy kitchen, storage space doubles as a play prop.

C) Three pegs hung 2 feet above the floor in a toddler's room provide a place for the child to hang hats and coats.

Getting More out of Children's Beds

Because children use their bedrooms for playing as well as sleeping, open area on the floor is often at a premium. To free up more space, try incorporating storage into the bed. There are also ways to work in extra sleeping space, perhaps for friends, siblings, or cousins.

Bunk beds. Consider stackable twin beds that can be used separately if your needs or space arrangements change. If there is no built-in storage space, add containers under the lower bunk. To provide a nightstand for the person in the top bunk, install bracket shelves or another type of system within easy reach, though not where it could be used as a step.

Trundle beds. These have a pullout mattress under the main bed. Some types also incorporate storage drawers or have a mechanism that allows you to raise the lower bed to the same height as the top, creating a king-size bed. That feature is particularly useful if you need to turn a child's room into space for adult company or if kids want to be able to whisper to each other during sleepovers.

Because trundle beds need to be pulled out and pushed in, they must be used where there is clear space alongside.

Loft systems. These elevated beds keep floor space free for other things, such as a desk or bureau. You can also construct a loft bed over another bed aligned at a perpendicular angle. This has the double-deck function of bunk beds but the bottom bed feels less confining.

Captain's beds. These have one or more levels of deep drawers underneath. If the drawers extend the full width of the bed, either use them for storing bulky items such as quilts or sleeping bags or insert drawer dividers that break up the space. Otherwise, the drawers wind up with the same disadvantage as deep toy boxes: Things get lost in them.

A.

B.

C.

D.

E.

A) These built-in bunk beds mimic the semi-enclosed alcove beds traditionally found in Scandinavian countries. Besides giving kids a place to sleep and store their supplies, alcove beds inevitably seem to kindle kids' imaginations. One day this kind of bed can be a treehouse; the next day, it's a ship.

B) As a way to pack useful features into a child's room, this bunk bed setup is hard to beat. Besides arranging the beds so that both kids can sit upright without bumping their heads, it incorporates headboard storage for each child and additional space in drawers under the lower bed. Next to the lower bed there is enough room to tuck in a desk or bureau. A two-section corkboard covers the wall that closes in the bottom section.

C) Spacious drawers under the lower bunk are a good place to store bulky but lightweight items, such as winter jackets or sports gear. The drawers are large, so add drawer dividers for storing small items.

D) This shelf fits over the rail of a top bunk, providing the equivalent of a nightstand.

E) With a trundle bed, it takes just seconds to get a child's room ready for a sleepover.

Closets

A closet is the most important storage area in a bedroom. It's considered so essential that tax assessors and home appraisers often use its presence to define a bedroom. There are two basic types of bedroom closets: reach-ins and walk-ins.

Reach-in closets fit into a wall and have doors that open into the bedroom. To allow space for hangers and to prevent clothes from being crushed, these closets should be at least 24 inches deep. You need clear space in front so that you have room to get what you want. Ideally, allow 30 inches of clearance unless the type of door requires more. The closet's height usually matches that of the room's ceiling. But where ceilings are very

high, reach-in closets often stop partway up and are topped with a display shelf.

Walk-in closets are rooms or alcoves fitted with rods, shelves, racks, and perhaps even drawers. To allow space for clothes to hang on both sides, make the closet at least 6½ feet wide. If you've inherited one too narrow, consider hanging clothes on one side and putting shoes or other shallow items on the other. Because walk-in closets tend to be larger than reach-in closets, they hold more stuff. But they are less efficient per square foot because of the empty walkway space.

An island is a luxury possible only with large closets. Besides providing storage space, the top of the island doubles as a convenient place to set out garments or accessories.

A) Some reach-in closets extend past the door opening on one or both sides, creating dead-end space where good access is often difficult. Extending rods across this space makes it easily accessible and allows you to use the back wall of the closet for another purpose, such as a shoe rack. Just leave enough room at the back corners to get clothes in and out from the rods there.

B) To make maximum use of a closet, allow only enough distance below each rod for the clothes you want to hang there. In a man's closet, like the one shown here, most garments on hangers need only about half the available height, so you could hang two rods in the space normally occupied by one. This single change doubles the available space in that part of your closet.

C) Walk-in closets don't have to be all business. This one incorporates a small television, perfect for anyone who wants to prepare for the day's events or maybe just check the weather while deciding what to wear.

Designing Closets That Work

There is no "best" closet design. What's ideal for you depends on what you need to store. The best way to determine that is to take everything out, sort it by type, and get rid of what you don't wear.

Planning a reach-in closet. Develop your plan around the amount of hanging space you need. If you run out of room before you work in all the drawers or shelves you want, you can probably find space for those elsewhere in the bedroom.

■ **Horizontal space.** In brochures advertising closet components, each garment gets about 3 inches of bar space. While that may be ideal, most real closets are far more crowded. To calculate your needs, hang each type of garment with the spacing you think is realistic and measure how much rod space that takes. Add a few inches so you'll have room for a few new pieces.

■ **Vertical space.** To estimate how much vertical space each category needs, use the illustration on page 141. To check the numbers against your own clothes, you need to measure only the longest garment in each category. Measure down from the closet rod so you include the hanger space.

Also take stock of other items you want to store. Then measure the closet. You need the inside length, width, and height, plus the distances between the door and the walls on the right and the left. With these numbers, you can go to a store that sells closet accessories and ask for design help, or use the online planning tools that some companies offer. You can also work out a plan on your own. If you're a visual thinker, try cutting out scale rectangles for each category and moving them around.

Planning a walk-in closet. Follow the same initial steps as you would for a reach-in closet. When you get to the actual design stage, treat each side as if it were a reach-in closet. If the closet is wide enough to seem like

a room, you can also add storage on the back wall. But don't crowd the back corners or you won't be able to get things on and off the side rods.

Quick and easy closet plan. If you don't want to sort pieces and measure them, just estimate how much tall and half-height hanging space you need. For long garments, place the rod 60 inches high—72 inches if you have evening gowns. For short garments, set the top rod 80 to 82 inches from the floor and the lower rod about 40 inches up. In children's closets, rods should be 30 inches high for most kids 3 to 5 years old and 45 inches high for kids 6 to 12 years old.

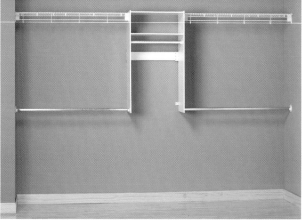

When you look at pictures of well-organized closets, it can be difficult to see how to translate the ideas to your own closet. One trick is to mentally delete the clothing and accessories that you see (top) and focus just on the skeleton of the system (bottom).

Coping with less-than-ideal closets. Some closets are too shallow to function well. The solution then may be to eliminate the door and create a storage system that opens directly into the bedroom.

Drawers and shelves don't require the 24-inch minimum depth that's needed for a reach-in closet (above).

Rods that extend outward work even where there isn't the 24-inch depth needed for standard closet rods (left).

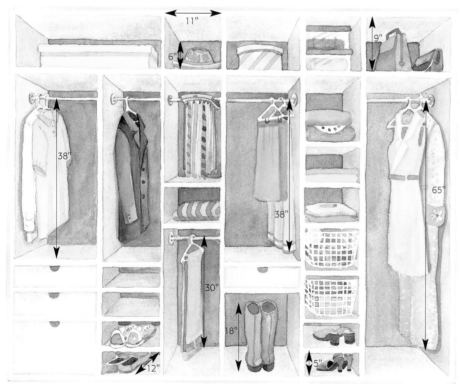

This illustration provides measurements that are based on average adult heights and styles of clothes. Use these as a guide, but check the measurements against your own clothing.

Deciding on Doors and Other Details

The kind of doors you choose on a closet influences more than just its appearance. The doors also affect the way you use space within the bedroom and in the closet itself. Sometimes you can transform an awkward closet simply by switching to a different style of door.

While some doors open wide and give you access to the entire closet at once, others slide over each other and never open more than halfway. Yet despite that drawback, these doors might still be the best choice for your situation. They don't swing out into the room, so they don't require a clear, deep path in front of the closet.

For the best of both worlds, consider pocket doors, which slide into gaps built into the walls next to the closet. Though these doors are usually installed when a closet is built, you can add them to an existing closet by sandwiching a new wall over the existing one. This dummy wall needs to extend only a little higher than the door, so you could end it there and top it with a shelf.

Bifold doors are another good compromise. Because they allow you to install narrower doors, they don't require as much clear space in front. However, they have twice the hardware that swinging or bypass doors need, so there is a greater risk that they'll fall out of alignment.

Most older houses and some new ones have high ceilings even in closets. If the ceiling in a closet is at least 9 feet high, you can add a third rod for short items. The rod shown here comes with a pull-down mechanism, which would allow you to use the highest rod without getting on a stepstool. Pull-down rods can also bring standard-height closet rods within reach of someone in a wheelchair.

Converting a Deep Closet into a Walk-in

If you live in a house built in the early 1900s, each bedroom may have one closet that you get to through a swing-out door. There's probably a shelf with a rod across the back and difficult-to-use spaces at the front on both sides of the door. If the closet is at least 5½ feet wide, you can more than double its storage efficiency. Take down the rod in the back and instead put rods on the sides. Have high and low rods on at least one wall. At the center back, add shallow shelves for shoes or purses. The center aisle will be a little cramped, but the closet is shallow enough that this shouldn't be a problem.

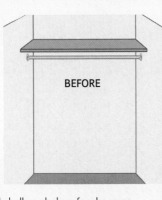

BEFORE

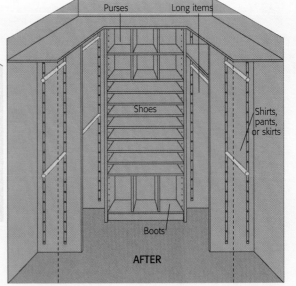

Purses Long items

Shoes

Shirts, pants, or skirts

Boots

AFTER

There's no rule that reach-in closets must have doors of standard height. Shorter doors increase storage space in this closet because they allow the drawers to extend all the way to the front.

Helpful Hint

In a reach-in closet with bifold doors, place any drawer units at the center so you can open them without any obstruction. If you have a reach-in closet with bypass doors, however, put drawers near the ends, as the middle space always has a door or two in front of it.

Closet Door Options

SWINGING DOORS
Standard, hinged doors provide full access but require an open path in front of the closet that's as deep as the doors are wide.

BYPASS DOORS
Suspended from a channel at top, bypass doors slide over each other so you never see more than half the closet at a time, and they don't jut into the room.

BIFOLD DOORS
These hinged-together doors usually have a pivot that slides in a top track. Allows for narrower doors, and nearly the full width of the closet is visible.

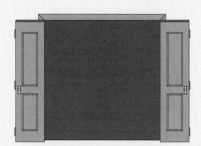

FULL-ACCESS FOLDING DOORS
Hinged together with support arm at top, these doors fold back onto nearby walls, providing full access to everything in the closet.

ACCORDION DOORS
Vertical pleats fold sideways, opening up most of the closet without needing much clear space; usually made of vinyl, sometimes topped with wood veneer.

POCKET DOORS
These slide into gaps (pockets) built into the wall, giving full access; end walls must be at least as wide as doors.

Storing Clothing

As you decide which clothes to store on hangers and which to fold and place on shelves or in drawers, you'll be guided partly by the storage space you have available. But you'll also want to consider which method will best preserve the shape of the garments and keep them from wrinkling.

Pants. If your closet is set up for longer garments, save rod space by hanging pants lengthwise from the cuff. Otherwise, fold pants over a sturdy hanger. Flimsy hangers sag under heavy pants, causing the fabric to bunch up and crease. Many closet systems feature special pants racks. They vary in quality, so check before you buy. Some are sturdy and have rubber rings or other features that keep pants from slipping off. Others bend easily or are so slippery that it's hard to imagine why they're better than hangers. Many pants racks feature bars open at the front so you can retrieve pants easily. Some hangers also offer this feature. One advantage of using separate hangers rather than built-in racks is that you aren't locked into the number of pants you can store.

Skirts. Use either clip- or clamp-type hangers. Clips are more secure, especially with thin skirts, but they can stretch some fabrics or leave indentations in waistbands. If skirts are thin, you can store a couple of them on each hanger.

Sweaters. Because knits stretch, sweaters fare best when folded and placed on shelves or in drawers. If you must hang some sweaters, select those with a tight knit and use padded coat hangers.

Shirts and blouses. Dress shirts and blouses belong on hangers. Standard ones work fine. T-shirts can be folded or hung. If you store folded shirts in a closet, thin slide-out shelves or trays work best because they allow you to have short stacks on closely spaced shelves.

Adding Slide-out Shelves

Slide-out shelves are a great way to store folded knits in a closet. Make the shelves from thin acrylic or plywood. Use a table saw or router to cut grooves in uprights for the shelves to slide into. Because the shelves pull out, you don't need to allow space between them for you to reach in and out. Space them with just enough room for a single bulky garment or a short stack of T-shirts. From the front, enough of each item is visible for you to go straight to what you want.

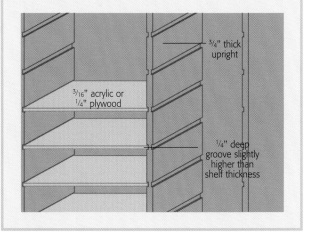

³⁄₄" thick upright

³⁄₁₆" acrylic or ¹⁄₄" plywood

¹⁄₄" deep groove slightly higher than shelf thickness

Closet-supply companies offer shelves that slide out on drawer slides.

Dresses. If a dress is made of slippery fabric, look for loops inside that you can slip over the head of the hanger so the dress doesn't fall off. If there are no loops, it takes just a few minutes to stitch in some made of ribbon. You can also use padded hangers or ones with a slip-resistant coating. Put dresses with thin straps on hangers that have indentations in the arms.

Suits and jackets. Always store suits and tailored jackets on wide hangers so the fabric doesn't stretch out of shape. With windbreaker-type jackets, you don't need to be so fussy.

Most pants racks are designed to hold one pair per bar, and the bars are nicely spaced so the pants aren't rumpled. While this gives you an incentive to avoid overfilling the closet, it also limits how you use the space. If a rack's capacity is eight pairs, for example, what happens when you buy a ninth pair? Unless you want to get rid of something, you're back to using hangers.

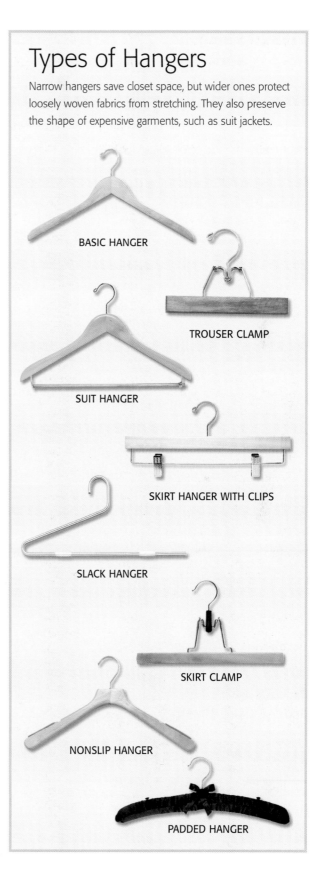

Types of Hangers

Narrow hangers save closet space, but wider ones protect loosely woven fabrics from stretching. They also preserve the shape of expensive garments, such as suit jackets.

BASIC HANGER

TROUSER CLAMP

SUIT HANGER

SKIRT HANGER WITH CLIPS

SLACK HANGER

SKIRT CLAMP

NONSLIP HANGER

PADDED HANGER

Storing Jewelry

One obvious place to keep jewelry is in a jewelry box on a bureau in your bedroom. If you need more space, you can outfit a shallow drawer with special compartments made for this purpose. To get more storage out of a single drawer, consider lift-out trays or double drawers, including those that are designed to hold silverware. If you use drawer dividers that are open on the bottom, slip a piece of felt underneath as a drawer liner. To keep a large collection of necklaces from tangling, hang strands on hooks. To attach hooks to the side of a cabinet or a dresser, use the kind with pull-to-release adhesive so you don't mar the furniture finish. Clip earrings to a piece of needlepoint fabric hung by a ribbon from a hook.

Storing Shoes

If you love shoes, finding a place for all of your pairs may be one of the more challenging storage issues you face. Before you design your bedroom closet around them, consider whether that is really the best place. A spot close to the front door might be better for everyday shoes, which may free your closet for dressier pairs.

If you don't have many shoes, you can line them up on a shelf or two. Slanted shelves make the shoes easier to see but take up more room. Also check out the wide array of shoe-storage systems available online or at home improvement centers.

Dimensions. Make sure your shoes will fit efficiently into the compartments. Athletic shoes for men and women, and dress shoes for men, occupy significantly more space than dressy flats. To minimize storage space, shoe manufacturers typically box shoes on their sides, nested toe to heel. If you follow that strategy in selecting a cubbyhole or box storage system, openings need to be at least 4 inches high by 7 inches wide for women's shoes with low heels, and 8 inches wide by $5\frac{1}{4}$ inches high for men's shoes. A 12-inch depth is usually enough.

Capacity. Shelves are more space efficient than boxes or pockets because you can butt shoes next to each other. For maximum efficiency, get a system with variable spacing between shelves. You may need just 3 inches for flats but 12 inches or more for boots.

Ventilation. Shoes need to air out after each use. Plastic boxes may be fine for long-term storage but not for sweaty shoes that you've just taken off.

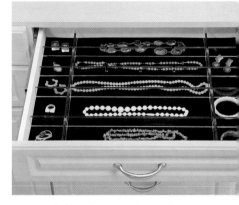

Drawer dividers bring order to a jewelry collection and help keep necklaces from becoming tangled.

A.

B.

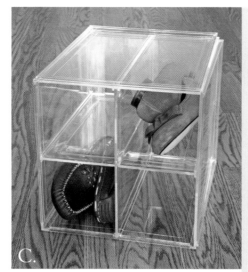

C.

D.

E.

A) Hanging shoe bags might be an option in a closet that has a rod and little else, but they aren't a good choice where rod space is at a premium. Another drawback is that the cloth tends to pick up dirt from soles.

B) Pocket organizers, often found in over-the-door models, store a lot of shoes in a small space. Pockets tend to be made of vinyl, which can smell, or cotton, which is easily soiled by shoe soles. This version is made of nylon, which stays cleaner. Like the other materials, it can be laundered.

C) Box organizers are neat and tidy. The compartment size is set, so make sure it matches your needs. At $5\frac{1}{2}$ by $5\frac{1}{2}$ inches, each of these cubbies stores a pair of loafers or sandals but holds just a single larger shoe, if that.

D) Loop-type racks keep shoes from being crushed. They work well on closet floors or shelves but they cannot be stacked.

E) Stacking shelves are available in a variety of styles, including ones with solid shelves and some with simple bars. You can add or remove sections as your needs change, though the spacing between shelves is fixed.

bathrooms

These days, bathrooms range from luxury spas to tiny closets. But other than powder rooms, bathrooms of all sizes share similar storage requirements. They need well-planned places for basics such as towels, toiletries, cleaning supplies, hair dryers, tissues, and dirty clothes.

Built-in cabinets. Except where there is a pedestal sink, bathroom storage usually starts with a cabinet known as a vanity. Countertops in kitchens tend to be a standard 36 inches high, but in bathrooms, there is more variation. The National Kitchen and Bath Association recommends heights of 32 to 43 inches, depending on the user's needs. Mostly that means tall people like vanities at the higher end of that range, while shorter people prefer them lower. But whatever your height, if you plan to sit down to put on makeup or shave, you'll find a low counter more convenient. You might even want counters at more than one height.

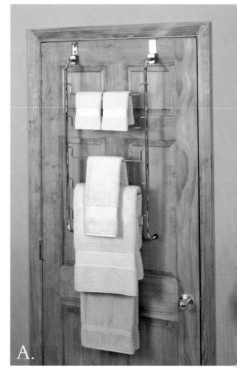

A.

In small bathrooms, consider cabinets that are 16 or 18 inches deep instead of the usual 21. If you need something even shallower, consider switching to a semi-recessed sink, which projects beyond the countertop. Some of these sit on cabinets only about 9 inches deep—not great for storage but better than nothing.

In larger bathrooms, additional built-in cabinets will give you more options for storing bulky things, such as towels.

Freestanding storage. If you have a pedestal sink or are looking for more storage but don't want to redo the vanity, consider adding a stand-alone cabinet or shelving unit. Models that fit over the toilet tank occupy almost no floor space but add many cubic feet of storage space. There are also many tall, narrow cabinets to choose from. Etageres, with slender columns and shelves that are often made of glass, are perfect for towels or baskets filled with toiletries. You might also consider a bench with storage underneath.

Shelves and other wall systems. These come in handy in most bathrooms and may be crucial if you have a pedestal sink and lack space for a free-standing cabinet. Near a pedestal sink, a wall-mounted shelf—or perhaps several levels of shelving—provides a convenient place for toothbrushes and other necessities.

B.

C.

A) In a tiny bathroom, even the back of the door can be used for storage.

B) This bathroom is small and simple, yet it stores all the essentials and even adds a nice extra touch: a place to sit down when you're pulling on socks. Spare towels fit under the bench, and there are dedicated places for toothbrushes and other personal care items—even a hook for the hair dryer. The large cabinet on the left holds supplies and toiletries.

C) Freestanding pieces are an easy way to add storage to a bathroom without embarking on a remodeling project.

Working Storage into Different Styles of Bathroom Cabinets

Wherever kitchen cabinets are sold, you can also find models designed as vanities for bathrooms. Just like kitchen cabinets, they are typically sized in 3-inch increments, usually from 18 to 60 inches wide and with various combinations of drawers and shelves. Drawers are generally more useful than shelves.

If you have room for a freestanding, furniture-style cabinet, you may also want a vanity that looks like furniture. Your choices range from styles that resemble antiques (above), to striking modern designs. The one constant is that furniture-style vanities have feet, or at least what appear to be feet in front of a deeply recessed toe-kick base.

D.

E.

A) The typical two-sink bathroom has a single countertop with storage below. This custom design divides the space differently. Between the two sink counters, the level dips a bit to a more comfortable height for sitting.

B) In the central cabinet between the two sinks in photo A, the cover lifts to reveal a mirror with jewelry storage below.

C) Standard cabinets were assembled to create high and low counters in this bathroom. The cabinets are rich with storage options, from shallow drawers to oversized shelves. The lower counter, an ideal spot for applying makeup, has its own small drawer.

D) Pedestal sinks look elegant and make small rooms seem larger but lack storage space. If you don't want to give that up, consider a wall-mounted cabinet. It also keeps the floor clear, which makes cleaning a breeze.

E) This is the same floating-cabinet idea but with considerably more storage space.

Adding Recessed Storage

Particularly in small bathrooms, taking advantage of space between wall studs is one of the best ways to add storage. You gain shelves or a cabinet without cutting into floor space. Step-by-step instructions for opening up the wall are on pages 26–27. Once you've done that, you can either install a ready-made storage unit or build a custom one.

Medicine cabinets. In older houses, the medicine cabinet over the sink was almost always fitted into the wall, and that approach still makes sense even though it is done less frequently. A recessed cabinet can have shelves nearly 4 inches deeper than one that is mounted to the face of the wall and still not intrude any farther into the room.

Behind-the-door storage. Another good place for recessed storage is the wall adjacent to the bathroom door. There is usually enough room there for shelves about 8 inches deep—enough for towels if you fold them appropriately. These shelves are also good for lotions and soaps, baskets filled with hair ornaments, and of course that bathroom staple: books.

Niches. Small recessed spaces can be handy in several places. Behind a sink, a niche might hold toothbrushes and a glass or maybe hairbrushes. By a toilet, it could hold books or tissues. And in a tiled wall around a tub or shower, a niche is a great place for shampoo.

A.

B.

C.

Niches can store lotions or tissues, thus freeing the countertop for other uses. The cubbies here also provide decorative effect.

A) In a small bathroom where only a tiny wall-hung sink fits, an inset shelf provides storage.

B) This bath is outfitted with three niches built into the wall behind the vanity, left open for storing towels. The niches are framed in oak-like wenge wood to mach the cabinet below.

C) Built-in shelves keep spare towels where they are easy to see and reach.

D) Projecting into the room no more than a standard mirror would, this recessed medicine cabinet provides much-needed storage above a pedestal sink.

D.

Organizing Bathroom Storage

Many people would never think of storing silverware without using a tray that keeps forks separate from knives and spoons. Yet in a bathroom, they toss the toothpaste, hairbrush, cotton balls, aspirin, and hair dryer into one drawer and get upset when it jams.

Kitchens have a lot to teach about how to solve bathroom storage problems. Drawer dividers, pullout shelves, and most other kitchen organizing solutions are just as useful in a bathroom.

A.

Add ledger here
if shelves have
a heavy load

When a toilet is boxed in on three sides by walls, adding bookshelves is easy. Just screw ledger strips to studs or drywall fasteners and then rest boards on top. Leave the shelves loose so they can be removed to give clearance for plumbing repairs. Besides books and plants, these shelves can store towels or other supplies.

Storing Tissue

The National Kitchen and Bath Association gives clear guidance about the best spot for locating a toilet paper holder: 8 to 12 inches in front of the edge of the toilet bowl, centered at 26 inches above the floor. When that won't work, just make sure the holder is within reach and in view. Where possible, store backup rolls where they are relatively easy for visitors to find.

Here's a good way to take advantage of space on the side of a sink cabinet.

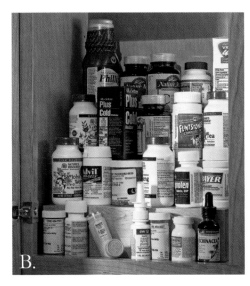

B.

C.

D.

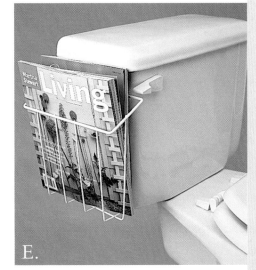

E.

F.

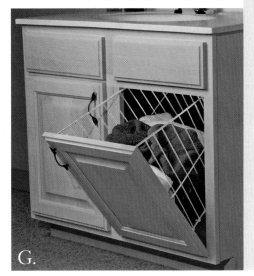

G.

A) Tilt-out drawers under a sink can store hairbrushes. Toothbrushes are OK too, as long as they are separated and there is enough air circulation so they dry.

B) Stair-step shelves allow you to identify even containers in the back row.

C) Sliding shelves, shaped to clear plumbing under the sink, corral cleaning supplies.

D) Pullout tray dividers put items in clear view and eliminate the need for drawers or shelves.

E) Auxiliary racks hold a variety of things, including magazines.

F) Door-mounted racks put otherwise unused space to use.

G) Vanity hampers store dirty clothes and allow air to circulate. Some tilt out, while others pull out on sliding shelves.

Storing Towels

Towels should normally be kept in the bathroom since that's where they will be used. But in tiny bathrooms, it may make more sense to move most of the spares to a room nearby. That frees up bathroom space for other essentials, including enough towel racks to go around.

Adding racks. To prevent musty odors, each damp towel needs to hang individually—ideally in a single layer, especially in humid weather. You can add capacity by replacing single towel bars with ones that have several fixed or swing-out bars. Some types even have a shelf on top for keeping a few fresh towels. Hooks are another option, but they don't allow as much air circulation around towels.

Keeping towel bars from wobbling. Drywall anchors are great for holding many things to walls, but they don't stand up to the repeated tugging that towel racks undergo. The racks need to be securely fastened to studs or to solid wood that is screwed to studs. Smart builders install horizontal pieces of framing, called blocking, around bathrooms before they put up the drywall. If you have a bathroom where this wasn't done, the easiest solution is to attach 1-by-4-inch wooden strips with 3-inch screws into studs all along the wall, as if you were putting up chair rail molding. Then screw towel bars to that (see illustration at right).

Even when a bathroom door is in the corner of the room, there is still almost always a gap of 4 inches or more between the door and the sidewall. This space can be used for a towel rack. The version shown here has loops that swing out from a pole and can be attached to door hinges, the doorjamb, or the wall.

A tall but narrow glass-front cabinet or set of shelves makes an ideal space for spare towels, especially in a guest bathroom. People can see what's available and help themselves without feeling like they are prying by opening doors. An open cabinet or one with glass doors also helps make a small bath seem a little roomier.

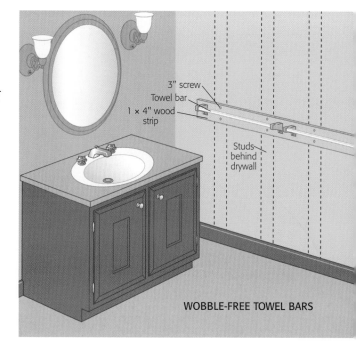

3" screw
Towel bar
1 × 4" wood strip
Studs behind drywall

WOBBLE-FREE TOWEL BARS

Adding Storage to Tubs and Showers

A variety of specialty racks help reduce the clutter of shampoo bottles and gooey soap puddles that tend to collect in showers or along tub ledges.

In a bathtub, consider a tray that spans the width. This lets wet washcloths and other items drip into the tub, where the moisture isn't a problem.

For a shower, the easiest solution is a rack that hooks over the showerhead. However, this puts it right where it will be doused every time someone showers. A better location is the wall opposite the showerhead, above where spray hits. But to mount a storage rack there, you need to either screw through the shower surround—which is often ceramic tile or fiberglass—or devise another method to keep the rack in place. If you must go through tile, buy masonry anchors to hold the screws. Though you can make the holes with a standard drill fitted with a masonry bit, a hammer drill with a carbide bit gets the job done much faster.

To reduce clutter, use small baskets or other containers to cluster products that you often use together, such as toothpaste, mouthwash, and dental floss, or a razor, shaving cream, and aftershave. If several people share a bathroom and each uses different shampoo, conditioner, and other products, consider the cluster approach to cut down on clutter by the tub. Put each person's items in a tote, and store the totes on a shelf between uses.

Helpful Hint

To avoid having to drill through tile to attach a storage rack in a shower or tub, hang the rack from an adhesive-backed hook that's designed to stay up until you pull a tab to release the adhesive's grip (see Resources, pages 188–189). You can buy caddies with this adhesive system already installed, or attach an adhesive-backed hook and hang a standard rack from that. Just watch the weight limit— $7\frac{1}{2}$ pounds for the biggest hook available. The caddy shown here weighs about 2 pounds, and each bottle of shampoo adds about 13 ounces. So you could load up this rack and still fall under the weight limit.

Shampoo bottles, bars of soap, and other supplies need to be within easy reach when you are taking a shower. But the moisture turns soap bars to mush and lifts labels off shampoo. The design of this shower eliminates those problems and results in an uncluttered look. At the far left you see the stainless-steel front of what the architect-designer calls a shampoo screen. Between it and the tiled wall behind, shelves open toward the side, providing sheltered but easily reached storage space.

home offices

A.

A well-organized home office can be a joy to use. By consolidating files, reference materials, a computer, and whatever other tools you need for your work, an office allows you to focus on tasks and complete them. That's much more satisfying than wasting your time looking for pencils or files that might be anywhere in the house. Most houses were not built with offices in mind, though, so the first step in planning a workspace is often finding a place for it.

Closet. If you can free up a closet, it may make an ideal home office. Closets are about 2 feet deep, which is also a good depth for a desk. Add shelves above and drawers below, buy a good chair, deal with wiring and lighting, and you're set. When you want to leave work behind, simply close the doors. If you want the office chair to hide too, make the desk a little shallower.

Space under stairs. This area often goes unused because it angles down to a height where a person can't stand up. But you may be able to tuck in a desk quite easily. The exact configuration will depend on whether the stairs go straight up or take a turn along the way. Whatever the plan, the interesting angles usually add to the charm of this type of workspace.

B.

Guest bedroom. This may be the best spot unless you tend to have long-term guests and work full time from home. To free up more room for the office area, consider switching the bed to a space-saving type, either a pull-down Murphy bed or a trundle bed that becomes king-size when you lift the lower section to the height of the main bed.

Dining room. With a little ingenuity, you may be able to add a home office to this room and still use it for dining, especially if you eat everyday meals in another space. Set up the office in an armoire or in an area you can screen off, and create enough storage space in the desk area. Don't use the dining table as a desk—it's not the right height. The table should not be your main office storage area either, though it's a good place to spread out a project while you're working on it.

C.

D.

E.

A) It's possible to tuck a tiny home office, complete with its own storage space, under a stairway. This solution works especially well in houses with high ceilings and stairs that turn. These features inevitably take up more space and therefore offer more storage opportunities underneath.

B) This sunny home office was designed to smooth over the conflicting demands that work-at-home parents face when they need to attend to business while also monitoring the kids. The desk area was planned with efficiency in mind. Above the desk, small cubbies hold supplies, and reference books are within reach. Below the countertop, file drawers and numerous shallow drawers provide abundant storage.

C) Most of the time, the wide, open doorway (shown in photo B) is an advantage because it keeps the parent working in the office within earshot of the rest of the house. But when hubbub in the kitchen threatens to drown out an important phone call, there's an easy remedy: Just slide out a wide door. Because it's mostly glass, family activities stay within view.

D) Even when you work from home, you may worry about feeling cooped up in an office all day and be tempted to position your computer in front of a window. The glare, however, can greatly increase eyestrain. A setup like this, with the window off to the side, works much better.

E) This home office is also the nursery. Baby supplies and toys take up a good part of the floor-to-ceiling cabinets. Office supplies are mostly hidden behind curtains. The elevated portion of the countertop makes for a convenient changing table.

Designing a Home Office with Storage in Mind

There is no one-size-fits-all plan for a home office. However, the design process is the same whether you are creating a full-time workspace in a dedicated room or setting up a small office that you will use just a few hours a week.

Few people start from scratch when they plan a home office. The first step usually involves sorting through papers, books, or other supplies to cull items you don't need. You should keep certain legal papers, but they might not have to occupy prime space in your office. Consider putting them in a plastic box with a tight-fitting lid and storing them in the basement or garage.

Once you have pared down, make a list of what you need to store and the jobs you need to perform. Then develop a plan around those.

Ergonomics first. Most home offices these days are centered around a computer. Even if you don't work full time from your house, if you think you may spend more than a few hours a day in front of the screen and keyboard, build your plan around a work surface that is the right height.

Regardless of the size of your home office, you may find it a challenge to keep the desk clear of clutter. One solution: Under the lower shelf, install a row of cubbies, which function much like the compartments in a rolltop desk. Size some openings for stacks of paper and others for miscellaneous supplies, such as scissors and a stapler.

Keeping a clear area under the desk is part of good ergonomic design because it allows you to stretch out your legs and shift your body position periodically. But in order to do that, you need to put the CPU somewhere other than its usual place on the floor under the desk. This office has a good built-in alternative.

Old-fashioned office desks are usually 29 or 30 inches high. That was fine when people tended to lean on their desks as they talked on the phone or wrote by hand. For paying bills or writing in a journal, these desks will still work well. But only people who are about 6 feet or taller should use them to support a keyboard and mouse. For that, you need a surface that is level with your elbows when your forearms and thighs are parallel to the floor and your feet are on the floor.

A keyboard tray, which pulls out from underneath a desktop, is one way to lower the working height of tall desks. In a home office that will be used by people of different heights, it's also a way to create a dual-height surface. A parent can use the keyboard and mouse on the desk, and a child can place them on the tray. Or you can install a tray on an existing desk that's too high. Be sure the tray is big enough so the mouse fits on it too if you want to avoid wrist strain.

Adding storage. Once you know the desk height, you can figure out how much space is left underneath for storage. Many people buy a desk on adjustable legs and add freestanding cabinets underneath. If you do this, consider getting base cabinets with casters so you can roll them out and clean behind them. Above the desk, add shelves or cabinets.

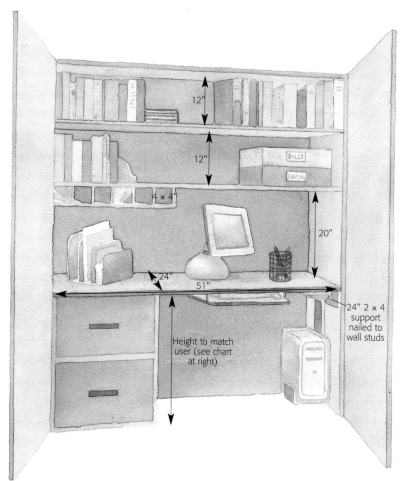

Create an office in an empty reach-in closet with only a file cabinet, a desktop, and bookshelves. When you're finished working, you can shut the doors and completely hide your office.

Work Surface Height

Person's Height	Desk Height
5'0"–5'3"	25"–26"
5'4"–5'6"	26"–27"
5'7"–6'0"	27"–30"
6'1"–6'5"	30"–32"

Pencils and pens. Office staples such as pencils, pens, tape, and paperclips used to go in a shallow drawer at the middle of the desk. Today, that space is often filled with a pullout computer tray instead. Storage alternatives include a desktop organizer or a side drawer with dividers. A combination approach often works best: Put pencils and pens in a mug on the desk and keep everything else in the drawer.

Paper. You can stack unopened reams of printer paper or stationery in a drawer, but shallow shelves work better for smaller quantities. Consider adding a series of cubbyholes below the lowest shelf, or get a desk organizer with multiple shelves.

Files. File cabinets or drawers are the backbone of many office storage systems. Be sure to consider capacity before you buy. Inexpensive cabinets are often quite shallow, so they don't provide nearly as much storage as more expensive, deeper units. If you are using a file cabinet under a desk, you won't save any floor space by getting the smaller unit; you'll just run out of space sooner. If price is an issue, you might decide that a used deep file cabinet is a better bargain than a new shallow one.

Before computers, desks were high enough to fit two file drawers underneath. Today, because of the lower height needed for working at a keyboard, it's more common to have a single file drawer and one or two shallower drawers. If there are two file drawers, the bottom one needs to be set close to the floor.

How to Build a Desktop Hutch

This freestanding hutch holds books, stacks of paper, and files. The measurements listed below result in a rack 42 inches long from just over half a sheet of ¾-inch plywood.

Use a tablesaw to cut the plywood into three strips 10 inches wide by 8 feet long. Then cut these lengths:

- 2 pieces 40½ inches (top and bottom)
- 2 pieces 18 inches (sides)
- 3 pieces 12¾ inches (vertical dividers)
- 4 pieces 9 inches (shelves)
- 1 piece 11½ inches (shelf)

1 Mark one vertical divider at 3¼, 4, 6½, 7¼, 9¾, and 10½ inches from the top. Transfer the marks to one end piece, but start ¾ inch up from the lower end to leave room for the bottom.

2 Place three 9-inch end shelves between the marks on the sidepiece. Attach them with 1½-inch finishing nails. Sketch centerlines if it helps you align the nails.

3 Nail the remaining 9-inch shelf to the back of the marked 12¾-inch vertical divider. This shelf should be 5 inches from the top. Nail the two assemblies together. Add the final shelf in the same way, 6¼ inches down.

4 Turn the hutch on its side and nail through on the bottom. Then flip the hutch and nail the top to the vertical dividers; also nail through the sides into the top. The sides extend above the top to create bookends.

A.

B.

C.

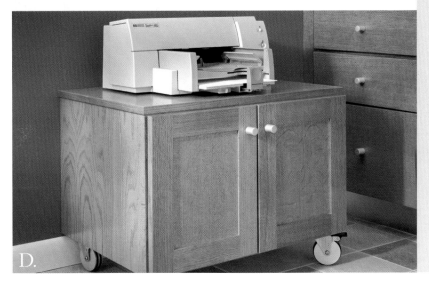

D.

Organizing Storage Within Your Office

Once you have your desk, drawers, and shelves in place, you can begin to put back the things you took out for sorting. Establishing a good organizing system from the beginning will save you a lot of time and hassle later and make it easier to keep your office neat and functioning well.

A) Magazine files can also store reports and other documents. If you want to create the most uniform look on your shelf, orient these bins with the tall ends out and label them. If you want to be able to add or remove magazines or papers without taking the containers down from the shelf, face the low sides out.

B) In a modern desk with a keyboard tray, a side drawer usually holds small items. But side drawers tend to be so deep that things get lost in them. To avoid this, install sliding trays or convert single drawers into doubles.

C) To keep items organized, use trays with small cubbyholes, like those for silverware. For some items, separate small containers may work better.

D) By placing a printer or other peripheral equipment on a wheeled stand, you can create an efficient U- or L-shaped office without having to deal with one of its usual consequences: a blind corner. When you need access to the nearby drawers, just move the printer stand out of the way.

Storing Books and Other Supplies

Well-designed bookcases and cabinets add to the appeal of any room and provide easy access to your collections. Shelves work well for books, maps, artwork, and many other items. Though you may decide to store some large volumes flat, or use a few piles as bookends, the shelf spacing should allow you to store most titles upright. In that position, books are easy to take out and put back, and you don't risk crushing the bindings. Store large paper items flat on shelves in base cabinets, which are typically much deeper than bookshelves.

Shelf dimensions. To store paperbacks, shelves need to be only 5½ inches deep and 8 to 10 inches apart. With hardback books, the spacing depends on the range of sizes in your collection and how you want to sort them. If you have mostly textbook-sized books and only a few art books, you might design shelves for the bulk of your collection and place the few oversized volumes flat or move them to a coffee table. If you have a more even mixture of sizes, you might want to design shelves for the larger ones so you can shelve all sizes together.

Organizing books. If you shelve books in a logical order, it's easier to find the titles you want. Use whatever system makes sense to you—it doesn't need to be the Dewey decimal system. For example, you might devote one shelf to travel guides and another to gardening books but not worry about the order of individual titles.

Protecting valuable books. Vintage books and expensive art books belong in the same rooms where people are, and not just to make it more likely that someone will open them. The moderate humidity and temperature of main rooms preserve books, while the excessive heat of an attic makes pages brittle. The dampness in a basement leads to musty smells and polka dots of mildew. Direct sunlight also damages books, so avoid placing bookcases where they face the sun. There's a lower risk, though, if you have high-performance windows with a coating that screens out ultraviolet rays.

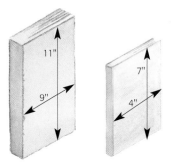

Books come in a variety of sizes and shapes, but you can use these dimensions as a guide. Shelves should be a little deeper than the books, as recessed volumes don't collect as much dust. To make books easier to remove, allow a couple of inches of headroom when you determine shelf spacing.

Closing Off a Bookcase

Open shelves are fine for books but not for things you don't want in clear view. If you don't have enough hidden storage space in base cabinets, consider adding doors to all or some of the shelves above your desk. So you can leave the doors open without bumping your head when you get up from your chair, consider doors that don't extend past the cabinets. These include sliding, tambour, fold-up, and fold-in doors, as well as simple window shades and curtains.

Made of slats attached to a fabric backing, tambour doors roll up like a window shade or curl up on a semicircular track.

Helpful Hint

If you use catalogs as reference material, store them near books on related topics. Place the catalogs in magazine files or baskets that fit on the shelves.

A.

B.

C.

A) A bookshelf system within reach of your desk chair keeps reference materials, computer disks, and other supplies where they are easy to find. The setup here includes a series of small drawers for little items plus five pullout trays that can be used as work surfaces or simply as places to open books.

B) Closely spaced slide-out shelves are a good place for oversized paper items.

C) It takes only a modest amount of bookshelf space to make a home office seem like a library, especially if you choose dark wood for cabinets and add a few classical details, such as furniture-style feet on base cabinets.

Creating a Mini Office

If you don't have room, or a need, for a large home office, you may still want a compact space where you can organize household papers or work at a computer. Having a set place, even if it's tiny and basic, saves you from having papers scattered all over the house.

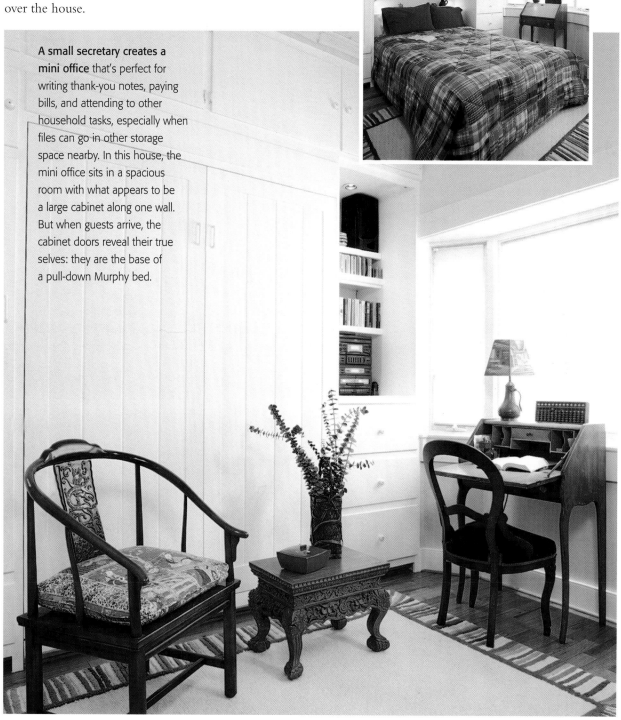

A small secretary creates a mini office that's perfect for writing thank-you notes, paying bills, and attending to other household tasks, especially when files can go in other storage space nearby. In this house, the mini office sits in a spacious room with what appears to be a large cabinet along one wall. But when guests arrive, the cabinet doors reveal their true selves: they are the base of a pull-down Murphy bed.

A.

B.

C.

D.

E.

F.

A) Outfitted with drawers, a counter, and a stool, an alcove off a hallway functions as a small home office for organizing mail and household papers.

B) Armoires accommodate an office in a piece of furniture, with doors you can close when you want work to disappear. Swinging doors provide a bulletin board surface or a spot to mount shallow baskets.

C) Built-in desks make efficient use of whatever small spaces there are—here a 4-foot-wide wall in an upstairs hall.

D) Wall desks hang like cupboards. The drop-down front doubles as a writing surface. This example includes cubbies, a drawer, an adjustable shelf, and a cork message board.

E) Secretaries are desks with shelves above. Add-ons may include a tilt-down table and an angled bottom shelf, perfect for storing large books.

F) Student desks have drawers and are a good height for writing by hand. In lieu of a standard pencil drawer, consider a pullout keyboard tray.

laundry rooms

L aundry rooms are all about work, but they can harbor fun activities too. If you plan carefully, you may be able to store all your essential supplies in a relatively small space and still have room left to fit in a sewing area or a small home office. At the least, you should be able to make doing laundry as efficient as possible.

Or you might want to take the opposite approach and look for a way to tuck a laundry area into another room of the house. For example, if you have a washer and dryer crammed into a tiny back entry where you need a mudroom, you might consider moving the machines to the spare bedroom that you now use as a crafts center. Besides freeing up the entry for another use, this strategy might save you work by putting the washer and dryer closer to where most laundry originates.

Open shelves below the cabinets in this laundry store detergent and other essentials within easy reach. Everything else fits above, out of sight.

Tucked-in Laundries

Instead of carting clothes to and from a laundry room on another floor or at the other end of the house, consider tucking in a laundry area near bedrooms. Look for suitable space in a large bathroom, an alcove, or a hallway along a stairway.

It's also possible to add a washer and dryer to a walk-in closet and still use it to store clothes. But this alternative comes with some important caveats. Remember that a laundry area is more than a washer and dryer; you also need a place to store dirty laundry and fold clothes. Vent the dryer adequately so you don't add humid air to the closet. And do a reality check: If your household generates a lot of smelly athletic wear or mud-caked gardening clothes, do you really want the laundry to share space with your clean clothes?

With some clever cabinetry, this laundry area fit into an angled passageway between a kitchen and a family room.

A.

A) Cycling clothes through the washing, drying, and folding stages leaves you with numerous short breaks. With a small desk in the laundry area, you can use this time to pay bills and organize other household activities.

B) Adding a sewing area to a laundry room makes a lot of sense, especially if your sewing consists mostly of mending or altering clothes. This sewing area has plenty of nearby storage, including tiny drawers for scissors, pins, thread, and buttons. The room also features a deep sink, which is ideal for watering house-plants as well as laundering delicate garments.

C) Laundry areas can double as mudrooms. In this house, stacking the washer and dryer saved enough space to allow a sink in the corner, generous base cabinets with clothes hampers, and cubbies for hats and jackets. Extending the cabinet below the cubbies created a bench where family members can sit to take off shoes or pull on rain boots, which stow away in the drawers below.

B.

C.

Planning a Laundry with Storage in Mind

To create an efficient laundry, you need places to wash, dry, fold, and maybe iron clothes, plus a way to store pieces that are headed into the wash or back to various bedrooms or closets. Kitchen designers think about the way a chef moves between food preparation, cooking, and cleanup. A similar process pays off when you are designing a laundry. Think through all the steps involved in doing laundry in your house and organize the supplies needed for each step so they are close at hand.

Many people use laundry rooms to store vacuum cleaners, brooms, and spare household items, such as light bulbs and paper towels. Unless you have other places for these, include them in your plans.

Choosing a Sink

A sink gives you a place to rinse away spills before stains set and to hand-launder delicate garments. It's also handy if you use the laundry room for crafts projects or watering houseplants. Though a utility sink on its own legs will do, you might prefer a built-in type. Consider one with a single large bowl, rather than two or three small bowls, so you can use it to wash things that might not fit in your kitchen sink.

A.

If you have a young child, adding a few kid-friendly attractions to your laundry area may do more for your efficiency than any number of cupboard organizers, although they help too. Hidden behind the cupboard doors in this laundry is an energy-efficient front-loading washer, as well as the dryer shown here. There is also space in the cabinets for hampers and laundry supplies.

Helpful Hint

Think about storage when you decide on a washer and dryer. You have a couple of options that beat the standard combination of a top-loading washer and a front-loading dryer. Energy-efficient front-loading machines with controls on the face fit under a counter, giving you additional space for folding clothes. Many of these machines also stack, and there are combination washer-dryers, which also have the dryer on top. One advantage of these options is that the dryer opens at a comfortable height so you can fold garments as you remove them. Units that you can stack or use under a counter also give you more flexibility if you move frequently.

B.

C.

D.

E.

A) Utility sinks with legs aren't actually freestanding. The bowl is mounted to the wall, and the legs just add stability.

B) An island can be as useful in a laundry room as it is in a kitchen. This island not only provides a place to fold and stack clothes but serves as a dock for a laundry cart that the owners wheel in from bedrooms. The design shields the mess from people coming and going through the back entry.

C) This arrangement gives you a no-mess way to dry a whole bowlful of hand-washed clothing. The towel bar is sturdy enough that you can place just-washed garments on hangers, accommodating many more pieces than you could on a clothesline. Drips fall harmlessly into the sink as the fabric dries.

D) Where there is a wall or cabinet on both sides of a sink, you can install a short length of closet rod.

E) Here a table serves as a clothes-folding station. Some people are most comfortable folding clothes on a counter that's standard kitchen height, 36 inches. Others favor tables, usually about 28 inches high. You might want to experiment to find out which works better for you. If you think you'll use the folding area for other purposes, such as crafts projects, go for table height if you plan to sit on chairs. For counter height, you'd need stools.

Storing Dirty Clothes

Though you may have a hamper in each bedroom, you still need a place near the washer and dryer to store dirty laundry that originates in other rooms. On washing day, you may need to sort and temporarily store piles of clothes in the laundry room.

Storing Laundry Supplies

If you buy detergent in bulk, consider installing a shelf so you can hoist the container once and then dispense into a cup the amount you need for each load. This way you won't have to lift the heavy container each time. Smaller jugs fit nicely into racks on the backs of doors or in sliding trays similar to those that fit under a kitchen sink.

A.

B.

Problem-Solving Kits

Even if you store scissors and sewing supplies in another room, consider keeping a mending kit in the laundry area so you can easily make simple repairs when you notice something needs fixing. This kit-type approach solves other problems as well.

■ **Repair kit.** Stock a basket or bin with scissors, thread in common colors, snaps and hooks, and any odd buttons you've found and are trying to reunite with clothing.

■ **Fabric-care kit.** Assemble any prewash stain removers you use, plus ingredients for treating specific stains, such as hydrogen peroxide, white vinegar, and baking soda. Add a lint brush, a chart detailing what various fabric-care labels mean, and a booklet or computer printout of stain-removal tips.

■ **Housecleaning kit.** The laundry is a good place to store supplies that you can carry from room to room. Fill a bucket or other tote with dusting cloths (microfiber types work best), a sponge, rags, old toothbrushes to use as mini scrubbers, and whatever else you use.

■ **Take-back kits.** Use the kit approach to store spare change, notes, and other things that you fish out of pockets before garments go into the wash. Consider having one small bin for each person in your household.

■ **Lost-socks kit.** Keep the strays in one place and you may eventually find their mates.

C.

D.

E.

F.

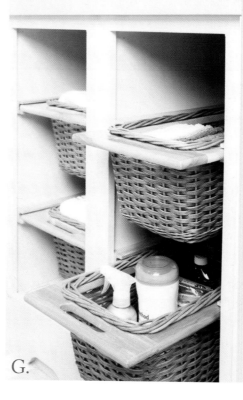

G.

A) **Consolidate cleaning supplies** in an easy-to-carry tote.

B) **A bamboo wine caddy** holds spray bottles of homemade stain removers as well as plain and scented water for ironing.

C) **Outfit base cabinets** with hampers that rest on sliding shelves.

D) **Suspended by ribbon** tied to wooden handles, a woven box provides a handy place to stash dryer lint.

E) **Wicker inserts** provide decorative effect on the upper cabinets in this laundry room, but you could also use them or other mesh inserts to add air circulation to cabinets where you store dirty laundry.

F) **Deep baskets** that pull out like drawers allow you to sort garments by color or care needs as you prepare to wash them.

G) **Baskets on sliding shelves** give you ready access to cleaning products.

Storing Ironing Tools

If you use your ironing board only occasionally, you may wonder sometimes whether it's worth all the space it takes. Luckily, there are other options, including smaller boards and fold-away models that fit into wall cabinets or even drawers.

But before you change your current setup, consider that fold-away ironing boards cost more than freestanding types and can be used only in the room where they are installed. If you like to watch TV as you iron and don't have a TV in the laundry room, you might be happier sticking with what you have now.

If you do opt for a fold-away, get one that holds steady as you maneuver the hot iron. Boards that fold down from the wall work well, as do most types that fold out from what appear to be drawers in base cabinets. Some base-cabinet models, though, have a single support rod in the center and are likely to wobble and tip. Boards with two supports are more solid. Because you can't just pick up and move a fold-out board, you'll want to make sure you'll be able to stand on the side you prefer. If your body will block light from the room's main fixture, also plan for adequate task lighting.

Built-in ironing boards fold out from wall cabinets, which are often recessed between studs. This allows the cabinets to project only slightly yet still be deep enough to store an iron and a board. The model shown here includes an electrical receptacle and a hook for just-pressed clothes.

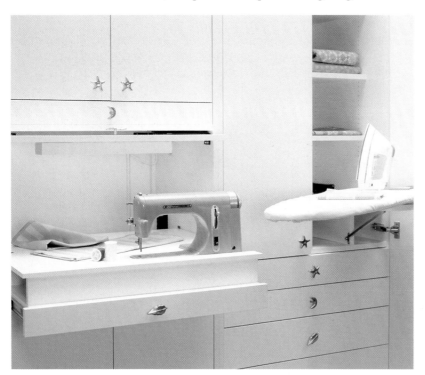

Convenience is everything when it comes to chores such as mending. This setup includes both a pullout shelf for a sewing machine and a pullout ironing board, plus plenty of storage nearby for necessary supplies.

Helpful Hint

To add hanging space near a dryer or ironing board, install foldout rods, known as drop hooks, on the filler strips between cabinets. Or mount the hooks to the sides of cabinets or to the wall. The kind shown here has small indentations to keep hangers from slipping. It stores a workweek's worth of shirts.

A.

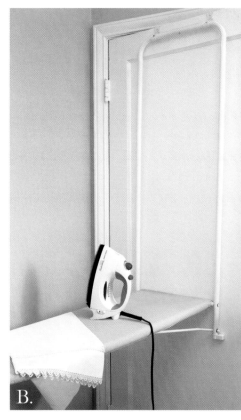

B.

C.

A) Ironing boards that fit into a drawer are hinged in the middle so they can be tucked into base cabinets. The version shown here slides out on heavy-duty glides, then pops up, thanks to a lift mechanism. This brings the board almost to countertop height, allowing you to stand the iron on the countertop between garments. If the countertop isn't heat resistant, provide a trivet.

B) An over-the-door ironing board is less expensive than a built-in folding one and more space efficient than a freestanding type. This model is a standard 42 inches.

C) If you prefer a freestanding board, you can store it on a holder that slips over a door or is screwed to a wall. This type stores an iron above the board.

crafts rooms

Good storage and plenty of work surfaces that have adequate light are the key ingredients in a crafts room. Because crafts projects tend to involve lots of small parts, you can put the full array of smart storage strategies to work. Use pullout shelves, drawer dividers, bins, and baskets to keep materials organized and make them easy to see and reach.

Work surfaces. A counter or table makes a good crafts workbench, provided you add seating that's an appropriate height. Use standard chairs for a table-height surface and stools for higher counters.

If you need additional space to store projects while glue or paint dries, consider adding a rolling cart with multiple shelves, or install folding shelves supported by collapsible brackets.

Storage. Most crafts materials are relatively easy to store as long as you keep them grouped and organized in some way. For ideas, check out the many solutions for storing spices (pages 114–115). A few materials present special challenges.

■ **Paper.** To keep large sheets from tearing or creasing, roll them around a cylinder, perhaps one you have saved from wrapping paper. Keep the sheets from unrolling by wrapping the cylinder with clear plastic wrap or shrink-wrap tape, or slip on the kind of padded elastic bands used to hold ponytails. You can also drape sheets of paper over wooden dowels that fit between notched brackets inside a cupboard or a niche.

■ **Brushes.** Never leave brushes soaking for long periods in a jar of water. Instead, store them clean, tip side up, in a jar or canister. Protect wide brushes by keeping them in their original sleeves, or make replacement covers from stiff paper.

A compact gift-wrapping center squeezes into a small laundry area. The counter provides work space, and scissors, tape, and other supplies fit into the drawer. A shelf with just enough headroom stores rolls of paper above.

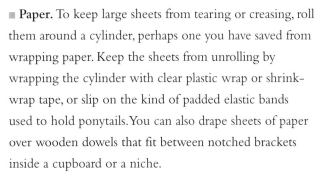

Bins are ideal for holding small crafts materials because you can see in and easily reach what you need. You can leave them out in the open, or hide a rack filled with bins behind closet doors. For storing numerous sheets of different kinds of paper, consider the same kind of wire racks that stationery stores use. Find these at companies that specialize in selling store displays.

A.

B.

A) This compact crafts area employs different strategies to store various materials. Vertical dividers in a tall cabinet store stiff paper, much like cookie sheets might be kept in a kitchen cabinet. Ribbons and paper hang on dowels that slip into curved grooves at each end. Cubbies above the desk and drawers underneath it store additional small items. A tall plastic trash can on a slide-out shelf keeps rolls of paper in good condition. Slide-out shelves hold other supplies.

B) With ample storage space, this laundry room doubles as a crafts center. There are plenty of shelves for supplies in baskets and pails. Numerous small drawers, often called spice drawers, hold little jars of paint, while tall compartments corral rolls of paper in baskets.

C) To work comfortably on a craft or potting project, you need seating of the right height. Stools work great in this room because the counter is typical kitchen-counter height: 36 inches.

C.

Designing a Sewing Room

Whether you have a large space and a passion for sewing or just a cubbyhole and an interest in simply mending clothes or making occasional presents, there are the same basic requirements: suitable surfaces for cutting, sewing, and ironing, plus storage for supplies, a good light, and a comfortable chair (preferably a swivel-type office chair on casters).

Work surface. For someone 5 feet 6 inches tall, the ideal height for a sewing table or counter is 28 inches, the same as most dining room tables. (Make adjustments for your height by adapting the chart on page 161.) Allow at least 18 inches of clear space to the left of the sewing machine so you have room for the fabric you are stitching. Set an ironing board to one side and a worktable on the other. Make them about 4 inches lower than the sewing table, if possible, so you can swivel your chair around and stay seated while you press seams or pin parts together. If you are right-handed, put the ironing board on your left. For cutting, counter-top height or even higher (36 to 40 inches) is better because you can work without bending.

Storage. The amount of storage you need depends on what kind of sewing you do.

■ **Tools.** If you use your sewing machine infrequently, keep it covered or in a closed cupboard, much as you might stow a mixer in an appliance garage. Or consider installing an appliance lift or a sewing machine lift (see page 112) and keeping the machine beneath a counter. Small tools, such as scissors, can go in a pencil tray, a canister toward the back of the sewing table, or on hooks or a magnetic knife rack on the wall behind the machine.

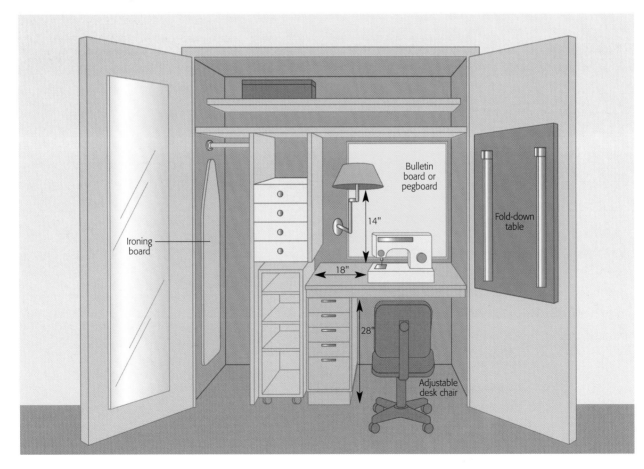

Ironing board

Bulletin board or pegboard

14"

18"

Fold-down table

28"

Adjustable desk chair

Thread. Make or buy racks with angled dowels ³⁄₁₆ inch in diameter—thin enough so you can slip spools of thread over them. Or sort thread by basic color families and store spools in clear boxes.

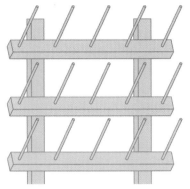

Notions. Keep buttons, snaps, and other notions in small jars or other clear containers so you can find what you need. Line up the containers on a narrow shelf toward the back of your sewing table, or store them on a revolving rack on a shelf. Solutions that work for spices (see pages 114–115) also work great for small sewing items.

Fabric. Protect fabric from fading by keeping it in closed containers or behind doors. To store pieces on shelves, fold the material and stack it so you can see a little bit of each kind. Or keep similar colors and fabrics in clear plastic boxes stowed away in cabinets.

Many kitchen cabinet accessories also come in handy in a sewing area. An appliance garage protects a sewing machine from dust when it's not in use. A pullout cutting board provides a handy surface for quick mending tasks, such as sewing on buttons.

Parts cabinets have numerous small compartments, usually with clear plastic covers, so they make good containers for buttons and other notions.

attics, basements, and garages

The biggest spaces in most houses are often the most neglected. Perhaps because they are out of the way of daily family life, garages, attics, and basements often become repositories for everything from outgrown clothing and broken chairs to valuable sports equipment and power tools. Yet when the junk is cleared out and the remaining items are stored away efficiently, creativity often flourishes in these places.

Attics

To determine whether you can use this space for storage, open the access door, poke your head through, and shine a flashlight around to see what kind of framing supports the roof. Truss framing, with relatively skinny pieces of wood fastened at various angles can't support weight at the bottom, which usually rules out using the attic. However, some trusses have a boxed-in area at the middle that's designed specifically to accommodate storage or even future living space, at least in areas where a load-bearing wall is underneath. Older homes don't have trusses but often do have 2-by-8-inch or 2-by-10-inch joists running across the attic floor. If you find these, you're in luck. If you're in doubt about your options, consult a structural engineer, an architect, or a knowledgeable builder for advice.

Store the heaviest items over load-bearing walls, which usually run perpendicular to roof rafters and floor joists. When you can't see joists, look at floorboards. They too run perpendicular to joists.

Pull-down attic stairs are safer and easier to use than a ladder. Most attic stairs fold out, but these telescope directly downward, so you can open them even if there is limited space below the attic access.

Attics and finished top-floor rooms often include spaces where the ceiling can't be high enough for a person to stand up. In this attic art studio, that space is put to good use with a series of cubbies that store art supplies and projects of various sizes.

Installing flooring. To allow even limited storage, you need a walking surface, known as a catwalk, over the insulation. Glue and screw wood spacers to the joists or the bottom chords of trusses so you don't compress the insulation. Over the spacers, install attic floor panels (see Resources, pages 188–189) or cut ⅝-inch-thick plywood to fit through the attic opening. To avoid creating a fire hazard, keep flooring away from exposed recessed "can" lights or where it might rub against wiring.

Storage strategies. You can usually suspend lightweight items from rafters. If your house is built with thick joists, you can also set lightweight boxes on the flooring. Because attics become hot in summer and cold in winter, limit storage to items that are not temperature-sensitive.

Basements

Moisture is the big issue in basements. Attend to any leaks before you add storage, and even once that's done, take a few simple precautions to make sure your things don't become musty and moldy.

Selecting shelving. Wire shelves work particularly well in basements because they allow maximum air circulation around stored items. A chrome finish also resists rust. Plastic shelves are another option. If you support shelves on wooden posts, put plastic cups under the feet. Or, for a more refined look, screw cabinet levelers or other metal legs to the posts.

Desiccants. You may wish to seal some items in plastic containers to protect them from moisture. However, they might still become musty because condensation can occur as the packed boxes cool down in the basement. Sealed plastic doesn't let even small amounts of moisture escape, so protect against mildew as you pack. To each box, add a little desiccant, a material that absorbs and holds on to moisture. To buy desiccant economically in bulk, ask at a pool-supply company for zeolite, sold as a filter material.

HOW TO MOISTURE-PROOF A BASEMENT CABINET

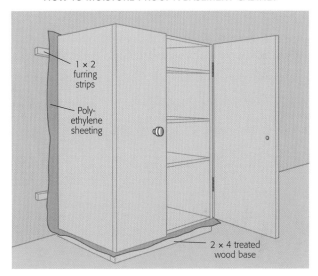

1 × 2 furring strips

Polyethylene sheeting

2 × 4 treated wood base

To protect a storage cabinet from moisture, build a platform of treated wood and attach furring strips to the wall. Spread a moisture barrier over the spacers and then lift the cabinet into place.

LADDER SHELVES

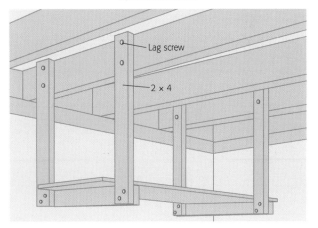

Lag screw

2 × 4

This approach keeps shelves away from the walls and the floor.

Garages

In many houses, the garage is the most practical place to store sports equipment, gardening supplies, car gear, and much more. The garage often also needs to serve as a home workshop and have space for a car. To make room for everything, take advantage of wall space and keep as much floor space open as possible.

The array of storage options from manufacturers may seem bewildering. Basically, though, the key decision you need to make is how you want to attach things to walls. Once that's set, you will probably be able to find a full range of hangers and other accessories to meet your needs.

Hooks. Individually or in assortments, hooks allow you to store pretty much anything: power and hand tools, wheelbarrows, golf equipment, and ladders. These hooks are inexpensive and just as effective as the more elaborate setups with fancy attachment systems. The main disadvantages are that you need to get out a drill or hammer each time you want to add a hanger, and, for heavy items, you can attach them only where there are studs. But you can easily work around the stud issue by nailing or screwing a horizontal board to studs, then attaching hangers to it.

Pegboard. Standard hardboard pegboard is inexpensive, easy to install, and adaptable as needs change. Steel pegboard costs more but is more durable and holds hangers more securely. Either type allows you to store gardening supplies near a potting bench or hand tools near a workbench. If the whole family uses a garage workshop, consider tracing around each tool with a marker so it's clear where each piece is supposed to return. See page 46 for installation tips.

Rivet shelving. No shelving carries heavier loads more economically than this type, which is probably why the same basic design is used in warehouses across the country. The heavy-gauge steel uprights have holes that allow you to tap the steel horizontal supports into place at whatever height you wish. The shelves rest on the metal, so they support hundreds of pounds, some more than 1,000 pounds, even when the actual shelving is particleboard. Angle-iron shelving has an industrial look and is usually used in garages and basements rather than in living rooms. Home stores carry a limited selection. For other sizes, shop at an industrial-supply store.

For each sport, there is probably at least one rack that stores all the related gear efficiently. Combination hangers often include baskets and hooks.

RIVET SHELVING

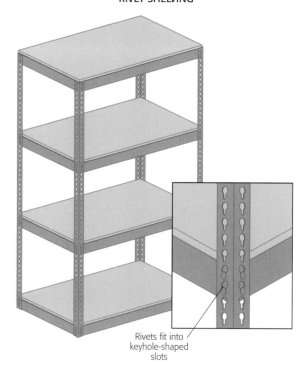

Rivets fit into keyhole-shaped slots

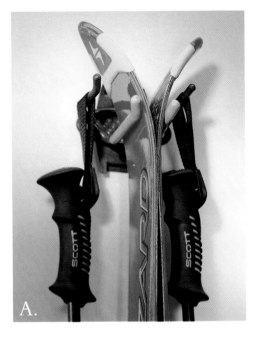

A.

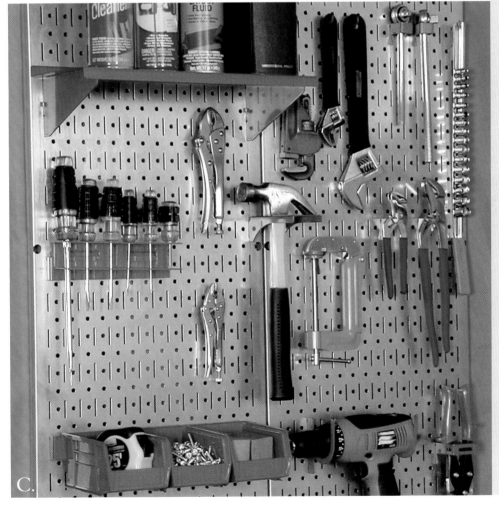

C.

A) This hook stores skis and poles, with enough room left for goggles.

B) A single hook on the ceiling holds a bike.

C) Metal pegboard grips tool holders and hooks more securely than standard pegboard does. This type is perforated with holes as well as slots so you can use different kinds of accessories with it, including standard pegboard hangers.

Slotwall. Many companies that specialize in installing whole-garage storage systems use plastic slotwall as a base. Once the panels are screwed to walls, it's easy to mount hangers, shelves, and even small cabinets.

Some companies sell their systems only through authorized installers, while others sell to consumers. The panels come in strips, often 12 or 15 inches wide by 8 or 10 feet long, so they are easier to handle than the 100-pound, 4-by-8-foot sheets of MDF slotwall used in retail stores. Some plastic panels can be attached so that fasteners don't show on the completed wall. With other types, you install panels by screwing through the grooves into wall studs.

Grid walls. In a garage, you can use a grid system in much the same way you would use slotwall. Numerous accessories allow you to hang tools or sports gear individually, as well as in baskets or on shelves. Get heavy-duty grids, with $\frac{1}{4}$-inch-diameter rods and welded connections, to support heavy items.

Rail systems. Think of rail systems as a single slat of slotwall or a single row of a grid system. You attach the rail to studs and then hook hangers or other accessories on at whatever points you wish. If you want accessories at different heights, install several rails, one over another. Be sure to check the weight limit, as rails look similar but are made of different materials.

Standards and brackets. This is probably the most common support system for garage shelving. With some types, you attach a top rail to studs and then hang standards from that. You may also be able to attach the standards themselves to studs or drywall anchors. Still other systems omit the top rail; you simply screw standards to studs. Shelves on fastened standards, with or without the top rail, can carry heavier loads. That is important for garage shelving, which tends to accumulate more stuff over time. Another way to add strength is to buy a system with standards that have a double row of slots rather than a single row.

A.

B.

C.

D.

E.

F.

G.

A) **Slotwall systems** allow you to attach hangers or hooks at any point, so they are ideal for storing small items individually. While shelf supports also fit into the slots, weight limits are relatively low, so you may want to support main shelves with a different system, such as standards and brackets.

B) **Standards are available** in different lengths, so you can keep shelves high on sidewalls where you don't want to scratch paint on car doors. On the end wall, shelves can extend lower.

C) **Rails carry small hand tools,** a shelf, and a stepstool in this garage. The wall cabinets, which are heavier, hang from several rails. Cabinets that are even heavier rest on the floor.

D) **With the right hook,** you can store even a wheelbarrow on a rail.

E) **Besides supporting shelf brackets,** standards can accommodate a variety of hooks, baskets, and other accessories.

F) **Rails are one of the least expensive** systems that you can reconfigure without tools. The ones in this garage support a few shelves as well as individual tools.

G) **Heavyweight grid systems** are strong enough to support bicycles, toolboxes, and garden tools.

Other Off-the-Floor Options

To add storage without using up valuable floor space in a garage, hang items from the ceiling or build platforms.

One prime spot for a hanging rack is over the track where the garage door rolls up. Wire shelving works particularly well here because it allows you to see what you've stored. Pulley systems are another option.

Platforms range from simple shelves that take advantage of otherwise unused space over the nose of a car to larger structures that qualify almost as separate rooms. In garages with high ceilings, platforms with stairs are a better choice than high storage reachable only from a ladder.

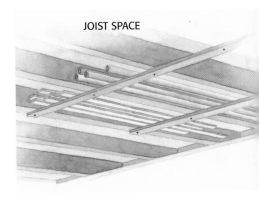

JOIST SPACE

If the ceiling is open, the space between joists is a good place to store thin materials such as wooden molding or pipe.

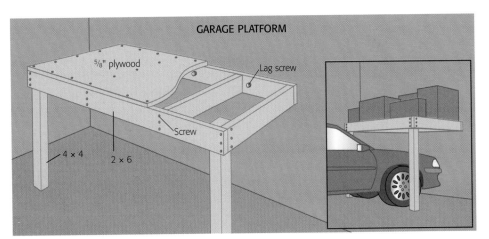

GARAGE PLATFORM

⅝" plywood
Lag screw
Screw
4 x 4
2 x 6

Size the platform and set its height so it will clear the front of the car and not hit the windshield. Use 4 by 4s for posts. If you plan to store heavy items, build the frame from 2 by 6s and use ⅝-inch plywood for the shelf. Attach the back to the wall with lag screws into wooden studs, or use masonry anchors if the wall is concrete block.

This pulley system works like miniblinds, with a built-in stop that keeps bicycles or other items up. A gentle tug releases the mechanism and allows you to lower a bike.

This type of overhead rack has openings as wide as 8 feet—useful for long or bulky items. The shelves hang 18 to 45 inches down from the ceiling and hold up to 500 pounds each.

How to Hoist Heavy Items

With this pulley system, two people can safely raise a heavy object, such as a game table, to the ceiling. Buy eight double-awning pulleys (ones with a pair of side-by-side wheels), four single-awning pulleys, and four eye screws.

1 Bolt four vertical supports to joists. Space them within the area where the heavy object will go.

2 Build a cradle from 2 by 4s. Size it to fit alongside the vertical supports, as shown.

3 Attach two of the single-awning pulleys near each other on a joist at the front of the cradle. Attach the other two to a joist behind the cradle.

4 Tie one end of a hoisting rope to an eye screw on a joist over the cradle, near one corner. Then feed the rope around each wheel of two double-awning pulleys. Repeat near the other corners of the cradle.

5 Each person should pull on one pair of ropes to hoist the cradle. Once the cradle meets the supports, anchor the ropes. Install a bolt and wing nut at each corner to take the weight off the pulleys.

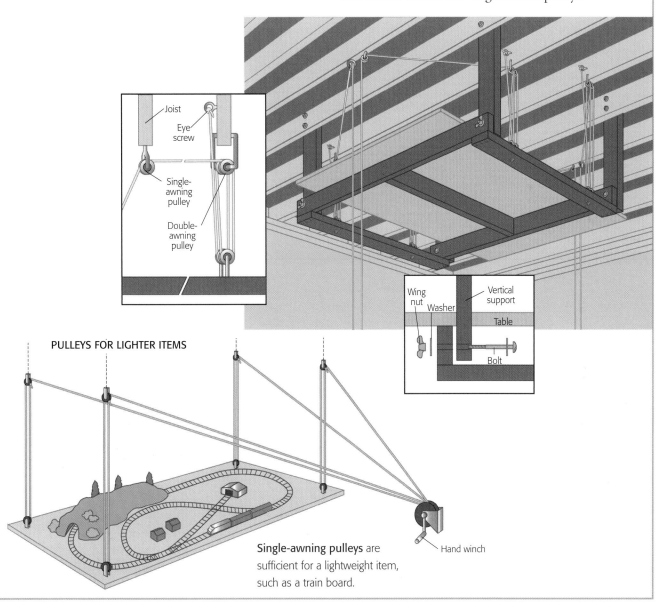

Joist

Eye screw

Single-awning pulley

Double-awning pulley

Wing nut

Washer

Vertical support

Table

Bolt

PULLEYS FOR LIGHTER ITEMS

Single-awning pulleys are sufficient for a lightweight item, such as a train board.

Hand winch

187

Resources

2 top left HomeCrest Cabinetry; 2 bottom left Ballard Designs; 2 bottom right Ikea; 3 top left Rubbermaid; 3 top right Knape & Vogt Manufacturing Co.; 3 bottom right Merillat Cabinetry; 6 top Wood-Mode Custom Cabinetry; 6 bottom Tigerman McCurry Architects; 7 top right Ikea; 11 top Ikea; 11 bottom left Design by Indian Rock Design/Build; 11 bottom right Liberty Hardware Mfg. Co.; 13 top and bottom Universal Designers & Consultants, Inc., design by Jane K. Langmuir, Inc.; 14 top and bottom Design by ShipShape; 15 top right Ikea; 15 middle right Rev-A-Shelf, LLC; 15 middle left The Container Store; 15 bottom Wellborn Cabinet, Inc.; 16 top Rev-A-Shelf; 16 middle Yorktowne Cabinetry; 16 bottom Maine Cottage; 17 top left Knape & Vogt Manufacturing Co.; 17 top right Bed, Bath & Beyond; 17 bottom Omega Cabinetry; 19 top left Scott Gilbride Architecture; 19 top right Ikea; 19 bottom left Wood-Mode Custom Cabinetry; 19 bottom right Rev-a-Shelf, LLC; 20 top Tichenor & Thorp Architects; 20 bottom Geoff Prentiss, Prentiss Architects. Cabinetmaker: Steve Phillips, Phillips Fabrication; 21 top left Robert Glazier, Hill Glazier Architects Inc.; 21 top right John Morris, Architect; 21 bottom Architect: Dale Gardon Design, Tamm Marlowe Design Studio; 22 bottom left and bottom right Myefski Cook Architects, Inc.; 23 top right Anthro Corp.; 24 top and middle Merillat Cabinetry; 24 bottom Lindy Small Architecture, Oakland, CA; 25 top Design by Peter Whiteley, construction plan available by searching under "hose bench" at www.sunset.com; 25 middle Ikea; 25 bottom left Dale Gardon Design, Tamm Marlowe Design Studio; 25 bottom right Design by Bille et Plume; 28 Rubbermaid; 29 top Ballard Designs; 29 bottom Rubbermaid; 31 top J.A.S. Design-Build, Seattle; 35 top right KraftMaid Cabinetry; 36 top Justrite Manufacturing; 36 bottom Rubbermaid; 41 top Design by Sherri Blume; 41 middle The Container Store; 44 top The Container Store; 45 top right Builder David Mulvaney, Annie Speck Interior Design; 45 middle John Silverio, Architect; 45 bottom Universal Designers & Consultants, Inc., design by Jane Langmuir, AIA; 46 Steel pegboard available from Wall Control; 47 top left The Lehigh Group;

47 top right Wall Control; 47 middle and bottom right Schulte; 47 bottom left Enclume; 48 Geoff Prentiss, Prentiss Architects. Charlie Feist, Feist Cabinets and Woodwork; 49 bottom Scott Gilbride Architecture; 52 top right Ikea; 53 top Andre Rothblatt, Architect; 55 top Geoff Prentiss, Prentiss Architects; 58 Studio Atkinson; 59 Design by ShipShape; 59 bottom left Ikea; 60 Cabinet doors and drawers available from Western Dovetail Inc. (www.drawer.com), Top Drawer Components (www.topdrwr.com), Valley Custom Door (www.valleycustomdoor. com), and Cabinet Door Shop Ltd. Co. (www.cabinetdoorshop.com); 61 top and bottom Wood-Mode Custom Cabinetry; 62 Stylist Emma Star Jensen; 63 top left Knape & Vogt Manufacturing Co.; 65 top left and bottom left Blum, Inc.; 65 top right Wellborn Cabinet, Inc. 65 bottom right Merillat Cabinetry; 66 top right Aristokraft Cabinetry; 66 middle right and bottom right Knape & Vogt Manufacturing Co.; 67 top Rev-a-Shelf, LLC; 67 bottom left and right Richeleau; 68 top Merillat Cabinetry; 68 bottom Rubbermaid; 69 top left KraftMaid Cabinetry; 69 top right and middle right Rubbermaid; 70 all Rubbermaid; 72–73 Tichenor & Thorp Architects; 74 top and bottom Myefski Cook Architects, Inc.; 75 top left and top right Myefski Cook Architects, Inc.; 75 middle Fernau & Hartman Architects; 75 bottom Kirsten Dumo, Satterberg Desonier Dumo Interior Design; 76 top and bottom Ikea; 76 middle Topdeq Corp.; 77 top right Ronald W. Madson, Madson Associates; 77 bottom left KraftMaid Cabinetry; 77 bottom right Charles Wooldridge; 78 Taylor Van Horne, Architect; 79 top left Jayne Sanders Interior Design; 79 top right Harry Teague Architects; 79 bottom right and bottom left Myefski Cook Architects, Inc.; 80 Michael Sant, Sant Architects; 81 top Scholz & Barclay, Architects; 81 middle Geoff Prentiss, Prentiss Architects and Joe Cooper, Ravenhill Construction; 81 bottom Nancy Barba, Architect; 82 Geoff Prentiss, Prentiss Architects. Cabinetmaker Charlie Feist; 83 Lane Williams Architects; 84 Avrack Inc.; 85 top left Avrack Inc.; 85 top right Custom Electronics; 85 middle Scholz & Barclay, Architects; 86 left Prentiss Architects; 86 top right Kajer

Architects; 86 bottom right Enclume; 87 top Scholz & Barclay, Architects; 88 Christine Curry Designs; 89 top right Elliott Elliott Norelius Architecture; 89 bottom Dale Gardon, Dale Gardon Design. Tamm Marlowe Design Studio; 90 Pepe-Lunche Designs; 91 top Diamond Cabinets; 91 bottom Dirk Stennick Design; 92 top Wood-Mode Custom Cabinetry; 92 bottom Merillat Cabinetry; 94 left Byon Kuth and Elizabeth Ranieri, Kuth/Ranieri Architects; 94 right Magnetic chalkboard paint available from MagnaMagic (www.magnamagic. com); 95 top left Sant Architects, Venice, CA; 95 top right Stylist Emma Star Jensen; 95 bottom right Aristokraft Cabinetry; 96 top Oasis Concepts; 96 middle Wellborn Cabinet, Inc.; 96 bottom Karin Payson architecture + design. Suzanne Myers, Elite Interior Design; 97 top Prentiss Architects; 97 middle Architect: Halperin & Christ, interior design: Sharon Low Hadley; 97 bottom Peter Kyle, Woodworks Construction & Design; 98 top Knape & Vogt Manufacturing Co.; 99 top left Diamond Cabinets; 99 top right and middle Richelieu Hardware; 99 bottom left Knape & Vogt Manufacturing Co.; 99 bottom right Blum, Inc. 100 top left Aristokraft Cabinetry; 100 top right Richelieu Hardware; 100 middle right Merillat Cabinetry; 100 bottom right Rev-a-Shelf, LLC; 101 top left Wellborn Cabinet, Inc.; 101 top right Richelieu Hardware; 102 top Ikea; 103 top left Knape & Vogt Manufacturing Co.; 103 middle Merillat Cabinetry; 103 bottom Interior design by Lorri Kershner; 104 bottom The Container Store; 105 top left Bed, Bath & Beyond; 105 middle and bottom KraftMaid Cabinetry; 107 top left Merillat Cabinetry; 107 middle and bottom left KraftMaid Cabinetry; 107 bottom right Aristokraft Cabinetry; 108 top HomeCrest Cabinetry; 109 top KraftMaid Cabinetry; 109 middle, bottom left and bottom right Knape & Vogt Manufacturing Co.; 110 top Enclume; 110 bottom Rogar International Corp.; 111 bottom David Coleman | Architecture; 112 top and middle Knape & Vogt Manufacturing Co.; 112 bottom Sewing machine lift available from Lee Valley Tools; 113 top left Wellborn Cabinet, Inc.; 113 top right Ikea; 113 middle Omega Cabinetry; 113 bottom Kitchens by Design; 114 top Bed, Bath & Beyond; 114 middle The Container

Store; 115 **top left** HomeCrest Cabinetry; 115 **top right** Merillat Cabinetry; 115 **middle** Wellborn Cabinet, Inc.; 115 **bottom left** Knape & Vogt Manufacturing Co.; 116 **top right** Dagan Design Inc.; 116 **middle right** KraftMaid Cabinetry; 116 **bottom right** Knape & Vogt Manufacturing Co.; 116 **bottom left** International Wine Accessories; 117 **middle** Organized Living; 117 **bottom left** Merillat Cabinetry; 118 Peter Brock Architect, Cabinets: Peter Witte, Witte Design; 119 **top right** The Container Store; 119 **bottom left** John Libby, Barnmasters; 119 **bottom right** Architect: Dale Gardon, Builder: Salcito Custom Homes; 120 **left** Wood-Mode Custom Cabinetry; 120 **top right** Merillat Cabinetry; 120 **middle right** Yorktowne Cabinetry; 120 **bottom right** Kitchen Craft; 121 **top left** Richelieu Hardware; 121 **top right** Georgie Kajer, Kajer Architects; 121 **bottom** HomeCrest Cabinetry; 122 **left** Buttrick Wong Architects; 122 **top right** The Container Store; 122 **middle right and bottom right** Knape & Vogt Manufacturing Co.; 123 **top left and bottom** Knape & Vogt Manufacturing Co.; 123 **top right** Wellborn Cabinet, Inc.; 123 **middle** Richelieu Hardware; 124 **top and bottom** Myefski Cook Architects, Inc.; 125 **top left** Siemasko + Verbridge Architects; 127 **top left** Rob Whitten, Architect; 128 **top and bottom right** Rubbermaid; 128 **bottom left** Maine Cottage; 129 **top** Rubbermaid; 129 **bottom right** Maine Cottage; 130 **top** Sean Parker, Bainbridge Architects Collaborative; 129 **bottom** Ikea; 131 **all** Paul Wanzer and Kim Munizza, Mithun; 132 **top left and bottom** Scholz & Barclay, Architects, TV lift available from Lift-Tech; 133 **top** Anderson Ultimate Bed; 133 **bottom** Brett Donham, Architect; 135 **top** Sally Weston, Architect; 137 **top left** Polhemus Savery DaSilva Architects; 137 **middle** Hardwood Artisans; 138 Myefski Cook Architects, Inc.; 139 **top left** The Container Store; 139 **top right** California Closets; 139 **bottom** Myefski Cook Architects, Inc.; 140 **all** Rubbermaid; 141 **top left** Knape & Vogt Manufacturing Co.; 142 **top** Rev-a-Shelf, LLC; 143 **bottom** California Closets; 145 **left** Knape & Vogt Manufacturing Co.; 146 **top** California Closets; 147 **all** The Container Store; 148 **top** Rubbermaid; 148 **bottom** Ikea; 150 **left** Merillat Cabinetry; 150 **top right and middle right** Myefski Cook Architects, Inc.; 150 **bottom** Wellborn Cabinet, Inc.; 151 **top** Sonia; 151 **bottom** Merillat Cabinetry; 152 **left and top right** American Standard; 152 **middle right** Kenneth Brown Design; 154 **top right** Knape & Vogt Manufacturing Co.; 154 **bottom right** American Standard; 155 **top left** KraftMaid Cabinetry; 155 **top right** Merillat Cabinetry; 155 **middle left** Ikea; 155 **middle right, bottom left and bottom right** Knape & Vogt Manufacturing

Co.; 156 **left** Hinge-It; 157 **top** The Container Store; 157 **middle** Bed, Bath & Beyond. Adhesive-backed hooks made by 3M, available at hardware stores; 157 **bottom** Luis Ibarra and Terese Rosano, Ibarra Rosano Design Architects Inc.; 158 **top** Prentiss Architects; 158 **middle and bottom** Mike Mora, Heliotrope Architects, Seattle. Amy Baker Interior Design, Seattle; 159 **bottom** Design by Kate Halfon Creations; 160 **all** Myefski Cook Architects, Inc.; 161 **bottom** HomeCrest Cabinetry; 163 **top left** Exposures; 163 **top right** KraftMaid Cabinetry; 163 **bottom** KraftMaid Cabinetry; 165 **top** John Gillespie, Architect; 165 **bottom** Myefski Cook Architects, Inc.; 166 **all** W. David Martin, Wm David Martin, AIA & Associates; 167 **top left** Bruce Teel, architect; 167 **top right and middle right** Ballard Designs; 167 **bottom left** L.L. Bean; 167 **bottom right** Maine Cottage; 167 **middle left** Bret Hancock, Thacher & Thompson Architects; 169 **top** Merillat Cabinetry; 169 **middle** KraftMaid Cabinetry; 169 **bottom** HomeCrest Cabinetry; 170 **left** EDI Architecture. Interior design by Pamela Pennington Studios; 170 **right** Swanstone; 171 **top left and top right** Jayne Sanders Interior Design Inc.; 171 **bottom** Myefski Cook Architects, Inc.; 171 **middle** Merillat Cabinetry; 172 **top** Rubbermaid; 172 **middle** Design by ShipShape; 172 **bottom** Merillat Cabinetry; 173 **top left** Design by ShipShape; 173 **top right and bottom right** Annie Speck Interior Design; 173 **bottom left** HomeCrest Cabinetry; 174 **top** Jayne Sanders Interior Design Inc.; 174 **bottom left** Design by Eurodesign Ltd. Drop hook available from Lee Valley Tools; 175 **top left** Liberty Hardware Mfg. Co.; 175 **top right** Target; 177 **top left** Merillat Cabinetry; 177 **top right and bottom** Tamm Jasper Interiors, Scottsdale, AZ. Cabinets by KraftMaid; 179 **top** Merillat Cabinetry; 179 **bottom** Rubbermaid. Thread rack available from June Tailor; 180 **right** Rainbow Attic Stair; 181 **top** Blue Ribbon Builders, Big Sky, MT; 181 **Attic floor panels available from Attic Deck (www.atticdeck.com); 182 **top** Rubbermaid; 183 **top left** Schulte; 183 **top right** Rubbermaid; 183 **bottom** Wall Control; 184 **top** Knape & Vogt Manufacturing Co.; 184 **middle** Schulte; 184 **bottom** Gladiator GarageWorks; 185 **top left** Rubbermaid; 185 **top right** The Container Store; 185 **middle** Rubbermaid; 185 **bottom** Garage Grids; 186 **bottom left** Bret Hancock, Thatcher & Thompson Architects, Santa Cruz; 186 **bottom right** Onrax Overhead Storage

Manufacturers and Retailers

Anderson Ultimate Bed, (800) 851-9213, www.ultimatebed.com

Anthro Corp., (800) 325-3841, www.anthro.com

Ballard Designs, (800) 536-7551, www.ballarddesigns.com

Bed, Bath & Beyond, www.bedbathandbeyond.com

California Closets, (800) 274-6754, www.californiaclosets.com

Diamond Cabinets, (765) 935-2211, www.diamond2.com

Enclume, (877) 362-5863, www.enclume.com

Eurodesign Ltd., (650) 941-7761, www.eurodesignltd.com

Gladiator GarageWorks by Whirlpool, (866) 342-4089, www.gladiatorgw.com

Hardwood Artisans, (800) 842-6119, www.hardwoodartisans.com

Hinge-It, (800) 284-4643, www.hingeit.com

HomeCrest Cabinetry, (574) 535-9300, www.homecrestcab.com

International Wine Accessories, (800) 527-4072, www.iwawine.com

June Tailor, (800) 844-5400, junetailor.com

Kitchen Craft, (800) 463-9707, www.kitchencraft.com

Knape & Vogt, (800) 253-1561, www.knapeandvogt.com

L.L. Bean, (800) 441-5713, www.llbean.com

Lee Valley Tools, (800) 267-8735, www.leevalley.com

Liberty Hardware Mfg. Co., (800) 542-3789, ww.libertyhardware.com

Lift-Tech, (661) 702-9055, www.televisionlifts.com

Maine Cottage, (888) 859-5522, www.mainecottage.com

Merillat Cabinetry, (517) 263-0771, www.merillat.com

Oasis Concepts, (949) 766-6360, www.oasisconcepts.com

Omega Cabinetry, (319) 235-5700, www.omegacab.com

Rainbow Attic Stairs, (407) 322-4622, www.RainbowAtticStair.com

Rev-A-Shelf, LLC, (800) 626-1126, www.rev-a-shelf.com

Richelieu Hardware, (800) 619-5446, www.richelieu.com

Rogar International Corp., (800) 351-1420, www.rogar.com

Rubbermaid, (866) 271-9249, www.rubbermaid.com

Schulte, (800) 669-3225,
www.schultestorage.com

Sonia, (888) 766-4287, www.sonia-sa.com

The Container Store, (888) 266-8246,
www.containerstore.com

The Lehigh Group, (610) 966-9702,
www.lehighgroup.com

Topdeq Corp., (866) 876-3300,
www.topdeq.com

Wall Control, (770)723-1251,
www.wallcontrol.com

Wellborn Cabinet, Inc., (800) 336-8040,
www.wellborn.com

Wood-Mode Custom Cabinetry, (877)
635-7500, www.wood-mode.com/

Yorktowne Cabinetry, (800) 777-0065,
www.yorktownecabinetry.com

Architects

Andre Rothblatt, Architect,
San Francisco, CA, (415) 626-5112,
www.andrerothblattarchitecture.com

Bruce Teel, San Francisco, (415) 957-9299

Buttrick Wong Architects, Emeryville, CA,
(510) 594-8700, www.buttrickwong.com

Dale Gardon Design, Scottsdale, AZ, (480)
948-9666, www.dalegardondesign.com

David Coleman | Architecture, Seattle, WA,
(206) 443-5626, www.davidcoleman.com

EDI Architecture, San Francisco, CA, (415)
362-2880, www.ediarchitecture.com/

Harry Teague Architects, Aspen, CO, (970)
925-2556, www.harryteaguearchitects.com

Hill Glazier Architects Inc., Palo Alto, CA,
(650) 617-0366, www.hillglazier.com

Ibarra Rosano Design Architects Inc., Tucson,
AZ, (520) 795-5477, www.ibarrarosano.com

J.A.S. Design-Build, Seattle,
(206) 547-6242, www.jasdesignbuild.com

Kajer Architects, Pasadena, CA,
(626) 795-6880, www.kajerarchitects.com.

Karin Payson architecture + design, San
Francisco, (415) 277-9500, www.kpad.com

Lane Williams Architects, Seattle,
(206) 284-8355, www.lanewilliams.com

Mithun, (206) 623-3344, www.mithun.com

Myefski Cook Architects, Inc., Glencoe, IL,
(847) 835-7081, www.myefskicook.com

Peter Brock Architect, Berkeley, CA,
(510) 524-2644, www.peter-brock.com

Prentiss Architects, Inc., Seattle, WA,
(206) 283-9930, www.prentissarch.com

Sant Architects, Venice, CA,
(310) 396-4828, www.santarchitects.com/

Scott Gilbride Architecture, Bend, OR,
(541) 388-3768, www.scottgilbride.com

Sean Parker, Bainbridge Architects
Collaborative, (206) 842-2011

Dirk Stennick Design, San Francisco, CA,
(415) 673-8640

Studio Atkinson, Palo Alto, CA,
(650) 321-6118, www.studioatkinson.com

Thacher & Thomson Architects, Santa Cruz,
CA, (831) 457-3939, www.tntarch.com/

Tichenor & Thorp Architects,
Beverly Hills, CA, (310) 358-8444

Wm David Martin, AIA & Associates,
Monterey, CA, (831) 373-7101,
www.davidmartinarchitect.com

Interior Designers, Consultants, Builders

Annie Speck Interior Design,
Laguna Beach, CA, (949) 464-1957,
www.anniespeck.com

Bille et Plume, Palo Alto, CA,
(650) 473-1232, www.billeetplume.com

Blue Ribbon Builders, Big Sky, MT,
(406) 995-4579,
www.blueribbonbuildersinc.com

Sherri Blume, www.jackandjillinteriors.com

Dagan Design Inc., (310) 396-2870,
www.dagandesign.com

Feist Cabinets and Woodwork,
Elk Grove, CA, (916) 686-8230

Jayne Sanders Interior Design Inc.,
Vancouver, WA, (360) 695-2279,
www.jaynesandersinteriors.com

Kate Halfon Creations, Martinez, CA

Kenneth Brown Design,
Los Angeles, CA, (323) 782-4307,
www.kennethbrowndesign.com

Kitchens by Design, Menlo Park, CA,
(650) 325-2060, kitchenbathstudio.com

Pamela Pennington Studios,
Palo Alto, CA, (650) 813-1797,
www.pamelapenningtonstudios.com

Phillips Fabrication,
Friday Harbor, WA; (360) 378-7199

Ravenhill Construction,
Friday Harbor, WA, (360) 378-5404,
www.ravenhillconstruction.com

Satterberg Desonier Dumo Interior Design,
Mercer Island, WA, (206) 232-1830,
www.satterbergdesign.com

ShipShape, Oakland, CA, (510) 533-0375,
www.shipshape.com

Suzanne Myers, Elite Interior Design,
San Ramon, CA, (925) 837-6688

Tamm Marlowe Design Studio,
Scottsdale AZ, (480) 423-3561,
www.tammjasperinteriors.com

Universal Designers & Consultants, Inc.,
Takoma Park, MD, (301) 270-2470,
www.UniversalDesign.com

Witte Design, Albany, CA, (510) 525-9321

Photographer Credits

T = top, B = bottom, L = left, R = right,
M = middle

Ron Anderson and Gloria Gale: 18B; **Ed Asmus:** 97T; **Margaret Barber:** 157BM; **Patrick Barta/Corner House Stock Photo:** 117TL, 153; **Brian Vanden Brink:** 4–5, 6B, 21TR, 23B, 23M, 45M, 81B, 81T, 85M, 85TR, 87T, 89TR, 101BR, 111TR, 119BL, 125B, 125TL, 127TL, 132B, 132TL, 133B, 135T, 137TL, 141TR, 165T, 168R, 180L; **Paul Carter:** 19TL; **Ken Chen:** 86TR, 121TR; **Grey Crawford:** 80, 95TL; **davidduncan livingston.com:** 176T; **Steve Dubinsky:** 81M, 158T; **Frank Gaglione:** 162 all; **Lois Gloor:** 137M; **John Granen:** 31T, 75B, 83, 111B, 130T, 131 all; **Ken Gutmaker:** 53T; **Jamie Hadley:** 97B, 97M, 103B, 113B, 118, 174BL; **Margot Hartford:** 11BL, 77TR, 91B; **Chipper Hatter/Corner House Stock Photo:** 136, 175B; **Alex Hayden:** 18T, 60, 85B, 89TL, 94R, 107TR, 143T, 158B, 158M; **Alex Hayden/Corner House Stock Photo:** 156TR; **Jeanne Huber:** 71 all; **Scott Jacobson/Corner House Stock Photo:** 152BR; **Kaskel Architectural & Kitchen Photography:** 22BL, 22BR, 79BL, 124T, 138, 139B, 150MR, 150TR, 160B, 160T, 165B, 171B; **Douglas Keister/Corner House Stock Photo:** 35TL; **Muffy Kibbey:** 88, 90; **Chuck Kuhn:** 8 all; **Jeff Mason:** 20B, 86L; **E. Andrew McKinney:** 52L; **Bill McNamee:** 41T; **Simone Paddock:** 49BL; **Charles Register/Corner House Stock Photo:** 23TL; **Ken Rice/Corner House Stock Photo:** 10, 111TL, 159T, 165M; **Richelieu Hardware:** 9T; **Jamie Salomon/Corner House Stock Photo:** 126B; **Michael Shopenn:** 77BR; **Alan Shortall/Corner House Stock Photo:** 7B, 7TL, 31B, 50, 66BL, 69B, 74B, 74T, 75TL, 75TR, 77TL, 79BR, 87TR, 101ML, 115BR, 117TR, 124B, 126T, 127B, 129BL, 134, 135BL, 137B, 137TR, 164; **Thomas J. Story:** 2ML, 15TL, 21B, 21TL, 24B, 25BL, 25T, 45TR, 49TL, 49TR, 58, 62, 75M, 79TL, 89B, 94L, 95TR, 117BR, 119BR, 119TL, 122L, 152MR, 163M, 166B, 166T, 167ML, 167TL, 170L, 171TL, 171TR, 173BR, 173TR, 174T, 177B, 177TR, 186BL; **Bill Timmerman:** 157BL; **Courtesy of Taylor Van Horne:** 78; **Michal Venera:** 96B; **Dominique Vorillon:** 20T, 72–73; **Roger Wade:** 95BL, 181T; **Jessie Walker/Corner House Stock Photo:** 101BL, 149; **Greg West/Corner House Stock Photo:** 103TR, 127TR; **Peter O. Whiteley:** 79TR; **Russ Widstrand/Corner House Stock Photo:** 42–43, 45TL, 125TR; **Michele Lee Willson (photo styling by Laura Del Fava):** 9B, 14B, 14T, 15ML, 17TR, 25BR, 38, 39B, 39M, 39T, 40, 41B, 41M, 44 all, 59T, 87BL, 87BR, 87ML, 101BM, 104B, 105TL, 105TR, 106T, 114T, 117M, 122TR, 135BR, 145R, 146B, 147 all, 157M, 157T, 159B, 172M, 173TL, 175TR; **Michael Winokur:** 59BR, 176B, 168L

Index

Alcoves, 54, 59, 111, 136, 137, 167
Appliances, 112–113
Armoires, 34, 76, 125, 134, 158, 167
Attic, 180–181

Basement, 181
Baskets. *See* Containers, baskets
Bathroom
    alcove, 21
    cabinets, 148, 150–151
    furniture, 148, 149, 150
    shelves, 21, 148
    tissue, 154
    towels, 156
    tub and shower, 157
Bedroom
    children's, 23, 25, 134–137, 140, 159
    guest (*See* Guest areas)
    nightstand, 126, 132, 136, 137
    reading light, 126, 131
    underbed storage, 128, 131, 132–133
Beds, 22, 133, 136–137, 158
Blankets and quilts, 136
Books and bookcases, 29, 31, 34, 38, 164
Breakfast bar, 96, 97
Built-in storage, 81, 86, 130–133, 148, 152–153, 186

Cabinets
    about, 18, 19, 60–63, 93, 148
    bathroom, 148, 150–151
    bedroom, 130
    corner, 22, 98–99
    dining room, 125
    doors, 16, 17, 113, 164, 173
    earthquake protection, 34–35
    entryway, 75, 76, 77, 79
    face frame vs. frameless, 62
    hardware and latches, 34–35, 38, 63, 90
    home office, 160, 165
    installation, 33
    kitchen, 22, 61, 67, 88–95, 98–101, 120–121
    latches, 34, 35
    laundry room, 75, 170, 172, 173, 174
    living room, 61, 62
    media, 61, 81, 82, 84, 85
    mudroom, 75, 78, 79, 169
    pantry, 120–121
    pullout units for, 7, 19, 92, 107, 113, 117, 121
    safety, 37
    salvaged, 30

standard measurements, 62–63, 93, 148
    toe-kick area, 20, 21, 63, 150
    updating, 90–91
Chests, 76, 126
Child safety, 23, 36, 38–39, 106
Cleaning supplies, 10, 100–101, 168, 171
Closets
    bedroom, 126, 138–147
    children's room, 134, 140
    entryway, 11, 75
    home office, 158
    reach-in, 138, 139, 140
    shelving, 54, 59
    standard measurements, 138, 140, 141
    walk-in, 138, 139, 140–142
Clothing, 129, 144–145
Collectibles, 23, 25, 34–35, 41, 87, 103
Computers. *See* Home office, ergonomics
Containers
    baskets, 16, 68–69, 87, 134, 172–173
    boxes and bins
    about, 16, 68–71
    archival-quality, 40, 41
    bathroom, 157
    bedroom, 128, 129
    children's room, 134
    craft supplies, 176, 177, 179
    home office, 29, 163
    kitchen, 105, 106
    laundry room, 68, 171, 172, 173
    for recycling, 53, 69, 122, 123
    wrapping paper, 128, 177
    garbage cans, 122–123
    hampers, 10, 38, 129, 155, 171
    stackable, 69, 70
    for toys, 38, 69, 134
Craft center and supplies, 71, 81, 169, 171, 174, 176–179
Cubbyholes
    for art and craft supplies, 177, 181
    children's room, 25
    entryway, 75, 78
    home office, 161
    for shoes, 75, 78, 130
    for wine, 117

Dining room, 124–125
Dishes and glassware, 15, 102–103, 119
Displays. *See* Collectibles
Doors
    blackboard and magnetic, 94
    cabinet options, 17, 113, 164, 173
    closet options, 142, 143

Door systems, 16–17, 100, 113, 120, 148–149, 155, 175
Drawers
    about, 64–67, 175
    bathroom, 154, 155
    bedroom closet, 138, 139, 141, 143, 146
    dividers, 14–15, 104–105, 107, 146, 155, 163
    double, 16, 17, 99, 105
    home office, 163
    kitchen, 7, 20, 103, 115
    load capacity, 64
    tilting, 100, 101, 154, 155

Earthquake protection, 34–35
Emergency supplies, 35
Entryways, 7, 11, 45, 74–79

Fasteners, 32, 156
Firewood, 86
Fold-down mechanism, 22, 23
Food. *See* Pantry
Furniture. *See also* Armoires; Beds; Tables
    bathroom, 148, 149, 150
    built-ins, 6, 24, 25, 87, 130–133
    cupboards and hutches, 7, 125
    dining room, 124, 125
    entryway, 16, 75
    home office, 131, 160, 162, 166–167
    salvaged, 31

Garage, 28, 59, 182–187
Garbage, 122–123. *See also* Recycling
Gift wrap, 128, 176, 177
Grid systems, 46, 47, 110, 184, 185
Guest areas, 126, 132, 136, 137, 158

Hangers and hooks
    bathroom, 157
    bedroom, 130
    children's room, 134, 135, 140
    closet, 144, 145
    entryway, 45, 75, 77, 79
    kitchen, 45, 106, 107, 108–109
    laundry room, 171, 173, 174, 175
    mudroom, 79
    for sports equipment, 47, 182, 183, 186
    types, 44, 142, 174
Hanging systems, 44–47, 140, 142, 186, 187. *See also* Pegboard

Hazardous materials, 8, 36–37
Heirloom and vintage items, 40–41,
    104, 164
Home office
    in borrowed space, 23, 124, 131,
        158, 159, 166–167
    desktop hutch project, 162
    ergonomics, 12, 160, 161
    salvaged furniture, 30
    shelves and wall units, 158, 159,
        161, 165
Hooks. See Hangers and hooks

Installation, making storage secure, 32–41
Ironing center, 174–175
Islands, 96–97, 111, 117, 138, 171

Jewelry, 146, 151
Joinery, basic, 64

Kitchen
    appliances, 112–113
    cabinets, 22, 61, 67, 88–95, 98–101,
        120–121
    counter height, 92, 93, 96, 178
    efficiency, 89, 92–93
    fold-up or fold-down items, 7, 22, 23
    hanging systems, 45, 46, 47, 55
    planning, 88–97
    pots and pans, 96, 108–111
    remodel, 90–91
    salvaged materials, 31
    under the sink, 100–101
    Universal Design, 12, 13
    utensils, 104–107
    wire shelving, 58, 59, 66, 67, 89

Laundry room, 14, 75, 168–175
Lift mechanisms, 112, 175
Living room and family rooms, 6, 80–87.
        See also Cabinets, living room; Media
Load capacity, 29, 50, 64, 180, 186

Magazines, 87, 155, 163
Measurements, standard
    books, 164
    cabinets, 62–63, 93, 148
    closet, 138, 140, 141
    counters and tables, 93, 148, 171, 178
    home office, 160, 161
    kitchen, 93
    pot rack, 110
    shelves, 12, 13, 48–49, 148
Media, 61, 79–85, 124, 131
Moisture control, 181
Mudroom, 75, 78–79, 169

Organizing the clutter
    bathroom, 154–155, 157
    board games, 86
    drawers (See Drawers, dividers)
    entryway, 11, 74, 75
    home office, 160, 161, 163

jewelry, 146, 151
laundry room, 172
principles, 9, 10, 112
Overhead storage, 181, 186, 187

Pantry, 118–121
Pegboard, 46, 47, 110, 182, 183
Pest control, 39, 40, 86
Pet supplies, 79, 97
Photographs and negatives, 40, 41
Pipe storage, 186
Planning. See also Measurements
    adaptability over time, 11, 29
    create new storage space, 18–30
    evaluation of possessions, 8–9
    getting the most for your money,
        28–31, 71
    maximize existing space, 14–17
    storage strategies, 10–13
Plastic
    bags, 123
    types, 40, 70, 71
Plates. See Dishes and glassware
Platform, garage, 186
Projector, for full-screen movies, 84
Projects
    booster shelves, 102
    desktop hutch, 162
    drawer divider, 104
    drawer insert for pot lids, 108
    garage platform, 186
    knife rack, 106
    plate rack, 102
    shelves over toilet, 154
    towel bar, 156
Pulley systems, 186, 187

Racks
    firewood, 86
    hat, 45, 77
    knife, 24, 106–107
    overhead, 186
    plate, 15, 102, 103, 119
    pot, 110–111
    shoe, 77, 147
    shower, 157
    spice, 17, 114, 115
    sports equipment, 182, 184, 185
    on toilet, 155
    towel, 19, 156, 171
Rail systems, 28, 45, 58, 59, 184, 185
Recycling, 53, 69, 70, 122, 123
Remodeling, 90–91
Retrofitting, 14, 66
Rolling storage
    carts, 6–7, 12–13, 96–97, 132, 171
    printer stand, 163
    shelves, 49
    underbed, 132
    universal design, 12, 13

Salvaged items, 30–31
Seating, storage under, 16, 25, 81, 86,
    127, 135
Sewing center, 169, 174, 178–179

Shelves
    adjustable, 30, 51, 58
    bathroom, 21, 148, 152, 155
    bedroom closet, 139, 140, 141
    book, 21, 81, 125, 131, 154, 164–165
    built-in, 6, 25, 48, 49, 127, 131, 152
    children's room, 134, 137
    closet or alcove, 54, 59, 144
    conversion kits, 14
    faux floating, 48, 58
    freestanding, 49, 57, 58, 59, 148
    hanging, 15, 55 , 58
    high near ceiling, 22, 23, 35, 95, 130
    home office, 158, 159, 161, 165
    kitchen, 58, 59, 66, 67, 89, 100, 109
    laundry room, 14, 168, 173
    load capacity, 29, 50
    for media, 15, 80, 81, 84, 85
    modular, 48, 58, 59, 116, 117, 119
    pull-down or swing-out, 24, 25, 66,
        67, 99
    rivet, 182
    as a room divider, 20, 21, 131
    salvaged, 30
    stair-step, 14, 15, 102, 103, 115, 155
    standard-and-bracket, 52–53, 58, 59,
        90, 184, 185
    standard measurements, 12, 13,
        48–49, 148
    support, 48, 50, 51, 53
    suspended, 181, 186
    universal design, 12
    vertical dividers in, 15, 63, 108–109,
        177
    wire, 58, 59, 181
Shoes, 10, 75–78, 127, 130, 146–147
Silverware, 104–105
Slotwall, 46, 47, 184, 185
Spices, 17, 24, 25, 114–115
Sports equipment, 47, 69, 182–186
Stairs, pull-down attic, 180
Stairway spaces, 18, 19, 25, 77, 158, 159

Tables, 7, 25, 117, 171, 178
Tools, 29, 47, 178, 182, 183
Toys, 38, 69, 81, 86, 134

Universal Design, 12, 13, 67, 142

Walls, 32–34, 55, 74, 75
Wall studs, 24, 26–27
Wardrobes. See Armoires
Weight. See Load capacity
Wheelchair access. See Universal Design
Wine, 7, 19, 116–117, 124